All About ADHD

The Complete Practical Guide for Classroom Teachers

By Linda J. Pfiffner, Ph.D.

SCHOLASTIC
PROFESSIONAL BOOKS

New York • Toronto • London • Auckland • Sydney

Cover design by Vincent Ceci and Jaime Lucero
Design by Joy Jackson Childs
Illustrations by James Graham Hale

ISBN 0-590-25108-2

12   11   10   9   8   7   6   5   23   7 8 9/ 9 0 1 2/0

Printed in the U.S.A.

Acknowledgments

This book is dedicated to:

- the staff of the school program at the University of California Irvine Child Development Center: David Agler, Jennifer Bain, Cheryl Crosswait, Daniel Flynn, Rose Holland, Kelly Passante, Cindy Vanderveen, and Dr. Ronald Kotkin, for sharing their many insights from years of teaching children with ADHD;

- Sarah Churchill, Donna Hall, Kathleen Healy, Norrie Hirsch, Karen Lerner, Shirley LaCroix, Fran Martin, Mary Olvak, Jay Teeman, and Suzanne Vighetti, teachers located across the U.S., for sharing ideas they found successful with their students with ADHD;

- Dr. Susan O'Leary, Dr. James Swanson, and Dr. Russell Barkley, mentors and supporters of my academic and clinical career;

- Terry Cooper who saw the need for this book, and the enthusiastic staff at Scholastic;

- Dr. Keith McBurnett for sharing his creative insights and clever ideas and for encouraging me through the process;

- and to the unlocked potential in every ADHD student who steps into a classroom.

Table of Contents

Foreword

As teachers know well, restless, inattentive, and impulsive behavior is common in children, particularly young school-age children, and especially boys. When parents or novice teachers express concern about such behavior in a child under their care, it may be wise counsel to encourage them to be patient, give time a chance, and wait for developmental maturation to work its magic at which time many children are likely to have outgrown these annoying or disruptive behaviors. However, if these behavioral problems have persisted for many months and seem excessive in comparison to most children, then concern for the welfare of such a child is very appropriate. Advising the parents and teachers of these children to simply ride out the behavioral storm is not only unwise, it may well be harmful to the future academic and social adjustment of such a child. When a child's levels of inattentive, impulsive, and restless behavior place him or her in the top 5 to 7 percent of normal children of the same age, have persisted for at least 6 to 12 months, have developed before age 12, and cannot be dismissed as intellectual delay, then that child is likely to have attention deficit hyperactivity disorder (ADHD).

Children with ADHD are subject to many risks, and many of these risks are school-related. Approximately 25 to 40 percent of all ADHD children will eventually be retained in grade at least once, be suspended or expelled from school, or fail to graduate high school. But there are ways to overcome some of the problems ADHD children face in school. As Dr. Linda Pfiffner explains in this book, one of the most powerful ways to help these children achieve school success lies in the classroom itself, in its structure and schedule of feedback, and in the teaching style and accommodation that take place there for a behaviorally disabled child.

Dr. Pfiffner has spent years developing and experimenting with new methods for assisting ADHD children in achieving greater self-control, will power, and academic effectiveness. Her experience includes years of working

within a school entirely devoted to ADHD children of elementary and middle school ages. She has consulted with countless teachers throughout the country and has published numerous studies on educational management of ADHD in peer-reviewed scientific journals. Her experience in working with ADHD children in the classroom is why I asked her to co-author a chapter on educational management for my own professional textbook on ADHD and for a similar chapter in my book for parents on raising a child with ADHD (*Taking Charge of ADHD,* Guilford Press, New York, 1995).

The methods for managing and educating ADHD children Dr. Pfiffner describes in this excellent and thorough guidebook have been shown to work in numerous scientific studies. Put simply, what is here works!

Russell A. Barkley, Ph.D.
Department of Psychiatry
University of Massachusetts Medical Center
Worcester, MA

Preface

During recent years, ADHD has captured the attention of many educators, mental health professionals, researchers, and parents across the country. Numerous research studies have been conducted and books have been written about the disorder. The increased recognition of the problems ADHD children face and the challenge they bring to the classroom seems to have fueled more and more questions about ADHD. I frequently conduct inservices and consultations in schools, and I invariably find that most teachers are eager for more information about the disorder and about how they can best work with ADHD students, particularly in regular education classes. My goal in writing this book is to bring together both the art and science of effective teaching for these students. Using the Parallel Teaching Model as the base for blending behavior management and teaching, I have drawn upon my own years of experience and research in model educational programs for ADHD students and the expertise and talents of many teachers and researchers across the country. The clinical insights and innovations of the teachers are found in actual "real-life" examples found throughout the book. These approaches have paved the road to success for many ADHD children. This information is intended to help you design strategies for your own classrooms, strategies that can help all your students be the best they can be.

Introduction

As an educator, odds are you have already encountered a student having Attention/Deficit/Hyperactivity Disorder, also known as ADHD. Even if you are just entering the teaching profession, odds are very high that you will encounter an ADHD student in your first or second year of teaching. An estimated 3 to 5% of the school-age population, over two million students, have the disorder. This translates to about 1-2 students in every class across the country. The impact of these students on the classroom is even greater than these numbers suggest. ADHD students are not easy to teach. Besides their primary problems of inattention, impulsivity, and overactivity, a myriad of social, academic, and emotional problems often accompany the disorder. Without help, ADHD can lead to years of frustration and misunderstanding.

This book is intended to help you prepare for these students. We know that classrooms and ADHD do not always mix well. The needs to focus, pay attention, and follow directions often go against the very nature of ADHD children. Some classrooms, such as those with a large teacher-student ratio, provide students with less attention than they need. A tenet of this book is that the problems ADHD children have in school are not due only to a disorder in the child or a problem in the structure of schools. Instead, these problems are aggravated by a mismatch between the classroom and ADHD students. The key to helping these students is to improve the fit.

Improving the fit can take several forms. In this book, the parallel teaching model will serve as the base. The parallel teaching model is a method for teaching ADHD students that interweaves techniques for increasing learning readiness and behavior management into the teaching process. From this base emanates a range of strategies and techniques. The parallel teaching model was designed for the regular classroom. Recognizing that many, if not most, ADHD students are being served in general education classrooms,

this model attempts to balance the individual needs of the few ADHD students in such classes with the needs of the larger classroom. This means helping all learners in the class, while providing the critical structure needed by the ADHD student.

As you proceed through this book, you may find that some strategies fit better with your classroom and teaching style than do others. Feel free to tailor the strategies to fit your needs. You may also find that many of the strategies sound like effective teaching tools for all students. In fact, many teachers report this to be true. They also say that in some cases they are actually easier to apply when they are used for everyone. We urge you to consider using the strategies for the benefit of all of your students.

Chapter One

Overview of ADHD

What Is ADHD?

ADHD, or Attention-Deficit/Hyperactivity Disorder, is a diagnostic term that describes a diverse group of children who have problems with inattention, distractibility, and, in many cases, impulsivity and overactivity. ADHD is recognized by the American Psychiatric Association and the United States Department of Education as a serious problem affecting thousands of students every year. Students with ADHD have trouble staying focused, listening, and completing work. Many create disruption in class by calling out, walking around the room during seatwork time, and socializing at inappropriate moments. While all children are inattentive, impulsive, or overactive at times, for ADHD children, these problems are much more extreme and enduring. These problems are so extreme that they interfere with the children's ability to function at home, at school, and to develop friendships. In other words, these are not children who occasionally have trouble concentrating and completing their work. These are children with chronic and impairing problems. These problems begin early in life, but are often not recognized until a child starts school. ADHD is far more common in boys than in girls; even so, thousands of girls have the disorder.

Many problems can look like ADHD but actually be another disorder. Being anxious or depressed can cause inattention; so can failing to understand the material

being taught. Some medications can also cause inattention and impulsivity. Distinguishing ADHD from such problems and from the normal range of children's attentiveness and activity requires a comprehensive evaluation by a trained professional. ADHD is not due to laziness, academic slowness, or poor parenting. ADHD is not something learned and it is not something kids choose to have. No one is to blame for ADHD. It is considered to be a neurological condition that usually requires special intervention. Although there is currently no treatment for the disorder, you, as an educator, can use strategies like those in this book to help these children be successful.

ADHD across the Lifespan

ADHD begins early in life. Most children with the disorder continue to have significant problems during adolescence and as many as one half are expected to have problems in adulthood (Cantwell, 1985; Weiss & Hechtman, 1986). The kinds of problems associated with ADHD usually change as one gets older. Some typical patterns are as follows:

Preschool: The first signs of ADHD often include high activity and the need for constant supervision in toddlerhood and preschool. Such children are accident prone, easily frustrated, and always on the go. Childproofing homes often becomes even more of a necessity than usual. These kids usually seek out the company of other children, but they often grab, push, and shove. Many experience their first school failures (including expulsions) at this time.

Elementary school: Sometimes, especially in the milder cases and the cases without hyperactivity, ADHD is not suspected until children start school. Then, in the face of having to follow an assortment of rules and regulations, the unrecognized disability is revealed. This is the time when ADHD is in its prototypic form. Assignments are often incomplete, report cards are often less than satisfactory, and peer rejection becomes the norm. Basic requirements like following teacher directions and classroom rules are not met.

Middle school and high school: As their peers are developing self-control and responsibility, the adolescent ADHD students continue to struggle in these areas. They are bewildered by multiple classes and teachers and can't seem to meet the expectations of their age. Their symptoms may become less extreme (especially the overactivity), but are still obvious when compared to their peers. Many don't make it through high school.

Adulthood: The good news is that a third to a half of adults who had ADHD as a child do quite well in the adult world. They may choose occupations like sales, entertainment, and business ownership, where their "symptoms" may actually be assets. However, another third, do not fare so well. They end up moving from job to job, often stay unemployed for long periods, and have more accidents, more divorces, and more arrests. A significant minority develop antisocial personality disorders and some end up in jail. Those with the least favorable outcomes seem to have had severe and chronic conduct problems in addition to ADHD as children (Barkley, 1990).

While diversity is the norm for ADHD and its course over the years, one thing is clear: ADHD is not outgrown. The key is to match environments to individual needs and strategically plan for adult outcomes. The answer is not to "wait and see."

The Subtypes of ADHD

ADHD is defined in the fourth edition of the Diagnostic and Statistical Manual for Mental Disorders (DSM-IV, 1994) published by the American Psychiatric Association. This manual is used to make diagnoses by medical and mental health professionals across the country. In the DSM-IV, characteristics (symptoms) of ADHD are divided into two categories: 1) inattention, and 2) hyperactivity-impulsivity. There are three subtypes of ADHD based on whether there are problems in one or both of these categories:

● ADHD-combined type where both inattention and hyperactivity/impulsivity are present;

- ADHD-predominantly inattentive type where only inattention is present;

- ADHD-predominantly hyperactive/impulsive type where only hyperactivity and impulsivity are present.

ADHD-Combined Subtype

ADHD-combined type is the "classic" variety of ADHD. Although these kids can be quite different from one another, they share the same core characteristics. Most don't pay attention well to group lessons or individual tasks (particularly repetitive, uninteresting ones). When they do attend, they often pick the wrong information to focus on. Many have a hard time starting and stopping tasks and shifting from one thing to another. They interrupt and call out in class, they can't seem to focus or stay quiet, and they are easily frustrated and bored. They often have difficulty regulating their emotions and may be prone to "outbursts." They are often "risk-takers" and disregard rules that don't meet their immediate needs. Assignments are often completed in haste. They can be fun-loving and engaging, but don't know when to quit. Many of these children are at risk for aggressive behavior and conduct problems. Repeated failure with peers and poor grades often chip away at the self-esteem of many of these children as they get older.

Here are some of the common problems of the ADHD-combined subtype:

Common problems in class:
overly active • doesn't sit still • too talkative • calls out without raising hand • impatient • fails to start work • work completed is sloppy • class clown • wants peer attention • doesn't accept consequences • easily frustrated • doesn't adhere to rules • noisy and disruptive • wants immediate gratification • difficulty persisting with uninteresting activities

Common problems with peers:
physically intrusive • touchy • butts into activities • easily frustrated • bossy • insists on own way • misses social cues • insensitive • can't see other's viewpoint • doesn't ignore provocation • wants to switch activities too often • rejected by peers

Common problems at home:

doesn't listen • rushes through or fails to complete homework • interrupts conversations • doesn't put things away • quick to temper when needs not met • forgets chores • dawdles in the morning • hates to wait • acts before thinking • reckless

Jason, age 8. Diagnosis: ADHD-combined type

Teacher's perspective: "Jason is one of the most enthusiastic, creative, and curious students I have had. Yet to get him to stay on-task and follow through on an assignment is a real challenge. I don't think he has completed an assignment all year. He usually ends up talking or bothering his neighbors when he should be working. He also doesn't seem to have learned the handraising rule: he calls out all the time. I guess you would have to say that he likes to be the "class clown" and act silly. He loves being the center of attention. He seems to be moving around all the time and has a hard time keeping his hands to himself. This is a big problem on the playground. Kids are always complaining about his behavior. I don't think he does these things on purpose or really understands the effect he's having on other people. He just seems to lack self-control...."

Parent's perspective: "Jason has always been very outgoing. He has a great sense of humor and sense of adventure. Nothing scares him. When most kids learn to walk, Jason learned to run, and he hasn't stopped since. He never would sit in his car seat. Now he never sits for a meal, not to mention homework. About the only things he does sit for (and for hours) are computer games and TV. I have to give him reminders all the time. Even to get dressed. Last night I told him to get in his PJs. He went up to his room. Twenty minutes later I found him playing with his toys. He's so easily distracted. I feel like I have to physically guide him through everything. Homework is usually a battle. Today, he finally remembered to bring home his math book, but he forgot the assignment, even after I reminded him over and over in the morning before school.

Sometimes it seems like he stores up his energy at school and lets it all out when he gets home. He's a nice boy, but his behavior makes me so frustrated."

ADHD-Predominantly Inattentive Subtype

Many children have ADHD-predominantly inattentive subtype, formally known as ADD without hyperactivity. These kids are not those usually thought to have ADHD because they are not overly active. In fact, they may be underactive or lethargic. These are kids who are extremely inattentive. They can't stay focused for long on a task and seem to spend inordinate amounts of time daydreaming. They are often quiet, and go unnoticed in a large classroom. They may seem to be "just lazy," but actually, they have great difficulty concentrating and controlling their streams of thought. They are very disorganized, forgetful, and need close supervision to get through a task. They seem to be confused about things like which page they should be on in the middle of a group lesson, or what their assignment is for home-work. It takes a lot of effort for them to shift their attention from one thing to another, just as it is hard for them to focus on any one thing for long. Work is often incomplete. These children may be more prone to anxiety and depression than are the impulsive, hyperactive ADHD children (Lahey & Carlson, 1991). They are often very aware of their problems and insecure about their abilities. Self-esteem is often low.

Here are some common problems of the ADHD-predominately inattentive type:

Common problems in class:

daydreams • doesn't complete work • forgetful • fails to attend to details • seems tired • "in a fog" • disorganized • loses things • messy desk • sloppy work • needs close supervision to stay on task • may have learning problems • great difficulty attending to task • easily distracted by internal and external stimuli

Common problems with peers:

withdrawn • quiet • ignored by peers • socially immature

Common problems at home:

homework not completed • chores forgotten • needs constant reminders • messy and disorganized • always losing things • spacey • doesn't seem to listen

Maria, age 11. Diagnosis: ADHD-predominantly inattentive

Teacher's perspective: "Maria is a hard worker and always has a positive attitude. She follows the rules and never disrupts the class. But I think she daydreams too much. It's like she's in her own world sometimes. She never seems to get the right assignment and has trouble finishing things on time. She seems slow. Her attention span doesn't seem to be long enough to complete anything. Maybe she's just not motivated. She's also very disorganized and loses her things a lot. Most of her work seems to end up crammed in the back of her desk or somewhere in the bottom of her backpack. She has a couple of friends, but she's shy and doesn't make friends easily. Her social skills seem to be a little young for her age."

Parent's perspective: "Maria has always been a sweet girl. She was an easy baby and rarely gave me any trouble. I didn't know anything was wrong until her teacher told me. But now looking back, she probably always had some trouble following through when I asked her to do something. She's so distractible. It seems like right after I've told her to do something she's already forgotten what it was I said. She leaves her stuff all over the house and seems to lose things constantly. Her bedroom is a mess. Recently, homework has become a problem. She tries her best, but ends up spending hours on her assignments. I think she's worried that she's not doing very well in school. Even so, she has a good attitude about things. She really loves her younger sister and likes being with the family."

ADHD-Predominantly Hyperactive Impulsive Subtype

This is a new subtype in the latest version of DSM. These are kids who are overly active and impulsive, but not currently showing signs of inattention. Because it is so new, researchers do not know a lot about this subtype.

About half of the kids with this subtype are in first grade or younger (McBurnett, 1995). Researchers think that many of these younger kids will start showing signs of inattention as they become old enough to encounter academic seatwork. This means many may meet the criteria for ADHD-combined subtype as they get older.

A word about severity: Along with differences in the types of problems they have, kids with ADHD differ in terms of the severity of their problems. For some kids, ADHD can be quite severe and disabling; for others it may be just a mild annoyance. Even the severity can vary from hour to hour and day to day. Problems may be virtually absent in some situations. Perhaps one of the most difficult things about the disorder is its variability. Teachers often comment, "He seems to do well on some days, and is even a model student at times. But then, for no reason, he falls apart." Parents often comment: "He can play computer games for hours. Why can't he pay attention to his homework for more than two minutes?" Remember, variability is part of ADHD. The conditions causing and affecting the disorder are not static. Also, don't interpret the behavior as being willful. If these kids could be successful every day they would be.

Problems that Occur along with ADHD

Many children with ADHD also have other problems such as oppositional behavior, anxiety, depression, or learning disabilities. If these additional problems are severe enough, additional diagnoses may be made along with ADHD.

ADHD and Oppositional/Conduct Problems

Over half the children with ADHD are also very stubborn, defiant, and aggressive (Barkley, 1990). When sufficiently chronic and severe, these problems make up a separate disorder called Oppositional Defiant Disorder (ODD). As suggested by the name, these are children who are overtly disobedient toward authority figures such as teachers and parents. They refuse to follow rules, and use temper tantrums and arguments to try to get their

way. They may seem to have a "chip on their shoulder" and appear chronically angry and resentful. Little things may set them off and they may constantly blame other people for their mishaps. The combination of ADHD and ODD is very challenging. Separating willful acts from unintentional disruption can be tricky. Even more disabling is Conduct Disorder which effects as many as 30% of ADHD children (Barkley, 1990). Children with conduct disorder have a pattern of breaking society's rules. They may lie, steal, run away, set fires, destroy property, or start physical fights. Often these symptoms don't emerge until the middle- or high-school years.

Michael, age 7. Diagnosis: ADHD with oppositional defiant disorder

Teacher's perspective: "When Michael entered my class, I knew he would be a handful. He was all over the room. He was loud and disrespectful. He made rude comments a lot and was always refusing to do things I asked him to do. He had a difficult time staying focused on his work and seemed to rush through his assignments. The most difficult part was dealing with his attitude problem. Little things seemed to set him off. The other children often became frustrated with his aggressive and bossy behavior, and he did not have many friends."

Parent's perspective: "When Michael has a good day, he's a joy to be around. He likes to have fun and be with lots of people. On other days, however, he can be a real challenge. I dread that I will get a call from Michael's teacher complaining about his behavior at school. He seems to have the same problems at school that he has had for years at home. He is defiant and has tantrums when he doesn't get things his way. He doesn't listen to anything I tell him to do and he argues over every point. He's also very active and can't seem to sit in one place for long. I've tried just about everything, but he seems to be immune to punishment. The neighbors complain about him because he's always getting into trouble. Michael has had so many problems, both at school and at home, I'm worried it's beginning to affect his self-esteem."

ADHD and Emotional Problems

Emotional disorders such as anxiety or depression also often accompany ADHD. Emotional disorders may arise independently or may be an outgrowth of ADHD. Kids with both ADHD and an anxiety disorder may be more disabled by the anxiety they feel than by the symptoms of ADHD. They are often overly and, at times, obsessively worried about things in their lives. Some kids worry about being apart from their parents. Others may worry about meeting new people or trying new things. Some may worry about what their classmates think of them or what their teachers think of them. The list of worries may seem to be endless. Sometimes these kids seem to manufacture things to worry about. They may also worry about their ADHD symptoms: forgetfulness, disorganization, etc. For some kids, anxiety may be expressed through acting out.

   Not surprisingly, many ADHD kids are also depressed. The repeated failures and frustrations experienced by these kids can take a toll. Even if the majority are not "clinically depressed," many are demoralized, feel poorly about themselves, and feel hopeless about changing their circumstances. Frequently, kids who are depressed appear to be chronically irritable or angry rather than sad. They may have lost interest in things they once enjoyed and they may avoid being around other kids. Their self-esteem is usually quite fragile. They often misinterpret others' actions and seem to have a veil of pessimism that continually colors their world.

ADHD and Learning Problems

As many as one out of three children identified with ADHD also have a learning disorder (DuPaul & Stoner, 1994). A learning disorder may be related to deficits in areas such as language processing, auditory processing, visual-spatial processing, or visual-perceptual processing. There is often confusion about the distinction between ADHD and learning disorders. Because ADHD can impair school performance, it is often thought to be a learning disorder. However, a learning disorder is defined by impaired performance on specific

standardized tests of language abilities, non-verbal abilities and/or achievement. If significant discrepancies are found between performance on such tests and overall intellectual ability, a learning disorder may be identified in one or more skill areas such as reading, mathematics, spelling, or language. These deficits are not simply the result of inattention; they constitute a separate processing problem.

There are many ADHD students who actually do quite well on standardized tests, especially if they are administered in a one-on-one setting, relatively free from distraction. However, many of these children still show serious academic problems in class. Their inattention to task, distractibility, and impulsivity interfere with their ability to complete work satisfactorily. Although these students may not have a learning disability, the quality and quantity of their classwork is seriously compromised by ADHD.

What Causes ADHD?

Current scientific theory and studies suggest that ADHD is a neurobiological condition (Barkley, 1990). The area of the brain that regulates impulses, attention, and behavior is thought to be underactive, compared to children without the disorder. There are likely to be many causes of ADHD, but none is well-understood. Probably the most frequent cause is heredity, although it is not known exactly what is inherited or how. We do know that ADHD tends to run in families. That means that many of the parents of ADHD children have ADHD themselves. It is likely that children often inherit the condition from one (or both) of their parents. In a smaller number of cases, ADHD may be the result of exposure to a toxin such as lead poisoning or complications during pregnancy or birth. Prenatal exposure to drugs or alcohol may also lead to ADHD-like behaviors. Contrary to what many people might think, diet (including sugar) does not appear to cause the disorder. We also know that social environmental factors don't cause ADHD. This means that parenting styles and teaching strategies do not play causal roles. However, external factors can have both positive and negative impacts.

Although social environments like the classroom don't cause ADHD, they can affect the severity of problems. We know that certain teaching styles are more helpful for ADHD students than are others. ADHD kids do well in one-on-one situations where there is lots of supervision and redirection to task. They also do well during novel, stimulating activities and in highly reinforcing situations. Take for example their attraction to computer games, which, much to their parents' dismay, they can play for hours on end. Computer games meet the basic requirements necessary to capture an ADHD child's interest: they are very stimulating and offer frequent, immediate positive reinforcement. The moderating effect of the environment on ADHD is good news. It means that you as a teacher can make a positive difference.

The Effects of ADHD on Teachers

The secondary demoralization often found in children with ADHD can also be found among their teachers! As most of you who have worked with an ADHD student know, it is demanding and may continually challenge your sense of competence as a teacher. The high rate of movement, interruptions, disruption, and talkativeness can be difficult to tolerate over time. You may find yourself giving the ADHD student more commands and directions. When met with resistance you may find yourself escalating in response. Feelings of frustration, anger, and hostility are not unusual. You may feel that you have exhausted your resources and are not sure where to turn.

One of the most important things to remember is: Don't take it personally! ADHD students are challenging even to the most seasoned teacher. They are often unaware of their most disturbing behaviors and when they are aware, they often can't seem to stop themselves. An intent of this book is to provide you with tools and techniques for handling ADHD students' behavior. Armed with these effective strategies, you can begin to enjoy the unique strengths of the ADHD child.

Many teachers who have worked with ADHD students for years and routinely use strategies discussed in this book actually prefer teaching these students over their "normal" counterparts. They like the sense of challenge and the sense of reward. Invariably, they report that these students have forced them to improve their teaching skills. Here are comments from several of these teachers:

"I like working with ADHD students because they are creative and full of curiosity."

"I'm never bored when working with ADHD students. I like the challenge of thinking of things I can do and ways I can teach to help them do their best."

"I like their energy— they're fun and entertaining in the classroom!"

There are many teacher characteristics that seem to be important when working with ADHD students. Teachers who seem to do well and enjoy working with ADHD students tend to be flexible, tolerant of individual differences, and interested in learning new teaching strategies. They often have high energy themselves and a strong interest in and commitment to teaching.

Educational Needs of ADHD Children

In thinking about the needs of the ADHD child, it is important to remember that ADHD is not a single problem. Some ADHD kids are hyperactive, and some are not. Some are oppositional, or anxious, or depressed; some are not. Still others have a learning disorder, but not all do. One word describes the educational needs of ADHD children: diverse. For the most severe, a small class with a small teacher to student ratio, is optimal. For the mild to moderate case, a number of accommodations to the regular classroom may be all that is necessary.

There are several theories about ADHD that have direct relevance for educational interventions. These theories describe neuropsychological deficits in ADHD, but as yet there is no consensus that any one theory accounts for the

disorder. These theories center around problems with inhibition and self-regulation, problems of arousal, and problems of motivation (Barkley, 1990). Difficulties in the brain systems for inhibition and self-regulation may explain why ADHD children have trouble inhibiting impulses, regulating their behavior according to rules and plans, and blocking out distractions. Difficulties in the brain systems related to arousal may explain why some ADHD children behave as if they are constantly trying to increase their arousal level by seeking stimulation and excitement. Researchers using brain-imaging techniques and psychophysiological techniques have documented abnormalities associated with ADHD that support these two kinds of explanations. Another theory suggests that there may be differences in the brain systems that process information about rewards and punishment. This theory does not have the same kind of evidence as do the other two theories as yet, but it explains why the kinds of rewards and punishments that work for most other students in the classroom are not sufficient to keep the ADHD student on track.

Considering ADHD from these perspectives helps us to identify educational strategies that are likely to be successful. The best strategies are those that change the classroom to promote greater stimulation, motivation, and regulation of behavior. The most effective classrooms include:

- structure: clear rules, routines, directions, and expectations
- salience: use of visual cues, prompting, repetition of instructions
- consistency: in limit setting, use of prudent corrective feedback
- motivation: frequent positive feedback and consequences
- interesting lessons: that capture the child's imagination and curiosity by using enthusiasm, creativity, and novelty

You will find each of these five themes in interventions throughout this book. As you proceed, remember that the intensity of the intervention necessary to help the ADHD child be successful varies with the severity and specific problems of the child. Try to build on a student's areas of strength rather than focusing only on remediation in order to foster self-esteem and growth.

Teachers who work effectively with ADHD children agree that it takes a lot of work, especially at the beginning. Expect to spend more time, energy, and effort in working with an ADHD student. You will need to be more involved with the student and the student's family. It may seem to be an uphill battle at times. But as one teacher noted, "the mountain was hard to climb, but reaching the top deepened my relationship with the student and my sense of being a teacher in a way that wouldn't have happened if the mountain had not been there."

Diagnostic Labels

Diagnostic labels, like ADHD, have many advantages. First of all, knowing a child is ADHD suggests the need for certain treatments and also may qualify the child for services that he or she may not otherwise receive. The ADHD label can also relieve children and parents alike. Knowing that they are ADHD helps kids realize that they are not stupid, even though they may have trouble paying attention or completing all of their work at school. Nevertheless, labels have many problems and limitations. Some kids who find out they have ADHD begin to think that they can't do well in school, or they start using it as an excuse. Self-esteem can suffer, because they think something is wrong with them. Some teachers and parents give up on a child who has ADHD. Some parents feel guilty because they think it is their fault. They may not realize that the problems ADHD students have can get better by making small changes in the classroom or at home. Finally, the label of ADHD does not describe the whole child. Kids having ADHD are very different from one another. Knowing a child has ADHD does not tell you about his or her unique strengths and talents, it does not tell you about his or her interests or dreams. Likewise, it does not tell you about the specific kinds of things that a child needs help in to be successful. It is usually best to focus less on labels and more on specific goals and behaviors. We may not be able to get rid of ADHD, but we can help students change certain behaviors and meet specific goals.

Chapter Two

ADHD in the Classroom: The Parallel Teaching Model

The parallel teaching model is a philosophy and attitude toward teaching that blends instruction and behavior management. For ADHD students, self-control and appropriate social behavior need to be learned. It is critical that you teach these skills as you would more academic material. Parallel teaching allows you to do just that. It involves setting up your classroom environment, and using instructional strategies and curricula formats in a way to facilitate a high state of learning readiness. Against this backdrop, parallel teaching involves making "interventions" an ongoing part of your teaching style. The term *interventions* means anything you do or say to redirect your students or keep them on track, such as giving clear directions, using praise, and giving corrective feedback. These interventions are delivered strategically throughout each lecture, group discussion, cooperative learning group, and independent work period. Used this way, they can become a natural part of your teaching style.

In this section, we first review strategies for increasing learning readiness in ADHD students through the way you design your classroom and through the

instructional and curricula formats you use. We then review interventions for managing attention and behavior that can be interwoven with your teaching.

Setting up the Classroom Environment

The physical arrangement of your class can either facilitate or impede learning opportunities and behavior management. With ADHD students, keep in mind the need for structure, clear physical boundaries, teacher proximity, visual stimulation, and minimal outside distractions. Consider the following recommendations:

Seat the student away from distractions and close to the teaching action.

In most classrooms this means seating the child:

- close to the front of the class (or by the teacher's desk or chalkboard) so that the teacher can continually monitor his or her work

- by peers who are good workers (not next to the child's best friend)

- away from the window, pencil sharpener, hanging mobile, door, or anything else that is interesting or distracting. If you teach in a less structured or eclectic classroom, seat the student away from the open, shared space.

Some teachers place their "problem" students at the "back" of the class, or in an isolated spot, often to limit their disruptive effect on other students. Sometimes this works well for kids who need more space. However, placement out of direct vision of the teacher usually creates problems. If you do have ADHD students away from your usual teaching spot, walk around the room every few minutes to make sure they understand the assignment and are working on it.

Organize seating to provide clear boundaries for students' work areas.

Individual desks with attached chairs are usually better than tables for doing independent seatwork. ADHD students often have difficulty with physical

boundaries and tend to annoy their peers by "getting in their space." Tables with many students do not usually provide clear enough divisions between students and tend to promote excess socializing. To facilitate group discussion and cooperative learning projects, individual desks or small tables can be grouped together in small clusters. Keep in mind that ADHD students may require more distance between their desks than do other students.

For the kindergarten ADHD student, seating arrangements during rugtime should also be carefully planned. The area in which the student sits on the floor should have clear boundaries. A carpet square often works well. You might also have the student sit next to you for close monitoring. Sarah Churchill who teaches second and third graders at Friends School of Atlanta in Decatur, Georgia, reports success in using a combination of large tables (seating four to six students), small tables (seating two students), and two one-person tables located in corners of the room and separated from the rest of the class by cubbies. Students who are distracted or having trouble concentrating on their work can choose to sit at a quieter small table or one-person table (which she promotes as being a privilege).

A note about standing: Many ADHD students simply cannot sit in one place for the time necessary to complete their work. Allow them to stand while working as long as they are not disruptive.

Have a well-organized classroom.

While most children and teachers benefit from an organized classroom, the benefits to ADHD children may be even greater. ADHD students typically have difficulty organizing their own space, are easily distracted, and seem to take advantage of (often unintentionally) any opportunity to go off-task. When given a direction to do something that involves leaving their seat (e.g., get materials, go work at a center), they often take the most circuitous route, and end up losing track of what they were told to do. If they do get to the right place, they are easily led astray by something else more interesting than the task at hand (e.g., colorful art supplies or pictures, a book, a bug on the wall), especially if they can't find what they need right away. To prevent these kinds of problems, keep centers uncluttered and in order. Have all the materials you need prepared each day before class. Keep supplies and materials stocked and in well-marked areas that you and/or your students can have easy access to. Color-coding books and materials can also be helpful. Also, use sturdy containers to prevent spills. Minor accidents (dropping a container of pencils or a stack of paper) can become a disruptive event for the whole class when an ADHD student is involved. Also, keep in mind that ADHD students often lose pencils, papers, books. Have plenty of replacements available.

Post prominent and interesting visual aides.

Bulletin boards can be a wonderful asset to learning. They are enhanced through use of color, relevant topics and examples, and student contributions. It was once thought that ADHD kids needed to be seated in white cubicles, free from any visual input. We now recognize the importance of novelty and creativity in the learning process. Feel free to create interesting visual displays. Have kids participate in creating the displays for each unit and post their completed work. Don't just post exceptional work of some students. Give all students a chance to post their best work and feel proud.

Ms. Fran Martin, at Paddock Lane School, Beatrice, Nebraska, teaches multicategorical students in grades K-5. She uses big charts posted around

"Superstar Work"

her room with inspirational messages for the students (e.g., 10 Steps for Feeling Good About Yourself, My Mind is Focused and I am Ready to Learn) *and* the teachers (e.g., Plan to be Positive). She likes to use lots of charts with words, since distractible students' eyes may wander and looking at the chart gives them another opportunity to read and learn.

Use bulletin boards to list classroom rules and behavior progress. Having rules posted (preferably on bright poster board with large block letters that can be easily seen from the back of the room) can reduce the need to repeat the rules verbally. You can just point to the rule. For example, at

the school program of the University of California Irvine-Child Development Center (UCI-CDC), periods of open talking, low-voice talking, and no talking, are designated through the use of signs showing either a "green light," "yellow light," or "red light," respectively. When the red sign is up and a student talks, teachers refer to the sign without having to continually repeat the current limits on talking. You can also arrange to use private hand signals to remind a student to stay on task or stop talking. Kids often respond better to a private reminder.

Behavior and assignment charts are also good tools for letting students monitor their own progress. These charts serve to remind students of the pro-

gram, and help remind teachers to be consistent too! Charts can be public or private. Many students respond better to private feedback on a small progress chart or checklist kept at their desk. This may be especially true for students who are having trouble. Public reminders may advertise their lack of success and lead to rejection, reduce self-esteem, and make the problem worse.

Instructional Strategies

You are competing with external stimuli (other kids, other things to look at) and internal stimuli (daydreams, thoughts about other things besides your class) whenever you are teaching. Capture your students' attention through interesting, well-planned, and well-paced lessons. Ms. Karen Lerner, a former dance instructor turned educator for special needs children at Prentice Day School in Tustin, California, likes to think in terms of "choreographing" her class for success. She finds that clear structure, clear rules, and advance planning go a long way in helping ADHD students choose the right steps. She keeps students apprised of daily routines, avoids surprise changes in the schedule, and limits down time. She likes to be proactive, rather than reactive.

Establish an effective classroom routine.

ADHD kids thrive in the midst of structure and routine. Having a routine helps kids organize their behavior and can be a great tool for preventing problems. Routines that work well:

- Having a schedule that you stick to. Post the schedule on the wall so that upcoming activities can be planned for.

- Teaching major academic subjects in the morning. Most kids (and teachers) are freshest at this time, which maximizes their learning and your energy and also allows for a range of natural activity reinforcers at the end of the day.

- Alternating between active and quiet activities, and between lecture, cooperative learning groups, and individual seatwork. Allow for move-

ment during and between lessons. Let students stand in the back of the room as long as you control the parameters.

- Alternating between high-interest and low interest activities. Have kids rotate through activity centers. Mr. David Agler, a kindergarten-first grade teacher at UCI-CDC in Irvine, California, draws an analogy to circuit training by referring to this as the "station-to-station work-out." He has students, working at their own pace, first complete the least desired activities and then move on to the more desired activities. Assignments or projects are checked before the student can go onto the next.

- Having routines for daily activities such as assigning and collecting work, handling homework, and making transitions between activities. Consider using charts that list the steps for various routine activities. Then have students review the steps before each activity. Such routines help ADHD students stay organized and focused on the task at hand.

- Teaching students what to do when they are done with their work early. Mr. Daniel Flynn teaches 4th, 5th and 6th graders at the UCI-CDC school. He instructs his students to start their homework when they are done with their classwork. Homework assignments are posted each day on a large board in the front of the classroom. Students just check the homework board and then get started on any of the assignments. Having students start homework during school allows them to ask questions if they don't understand something. Ms. Jennifer Bain, a second-third grade teacher at the UCI-CDC school, posts a list called "Things to do when you're done". The list contains ideas about things to read, draw, design, make, and write.

- Taking regular stretch breaks. ADHD students often become restless. When you notice this has happened, give the student an errand to run or a chore to do to expend the "excess" energy. They'll benefit from the break from sitting.

Deliver lessons in a style that maintains attention and interest.

Present your group lessons in a creative and engaging way. The more you can do this, the better attention and behavior you will see from your students.

- Scan and Deliver. Look around your class while you are teaching. If an ADHD student is drifting off, redirect and involve that student. If the ADHD student is listening, reinforce him or her.

- Use language your kids can relate to. Use examples that have meaning for them. Try to incorporate current fads (clothes, toys, games, food) and activities (going to the arcade, fast food) into your lessons.

- Bring "life" to your lecture. Try giving lectures as if you were a storyteller— raise and lower your voice, speed up and slow down your delivery, take on the role of one element of your lecture, and "ham it up" for a short while.

- Make sure that the most important points of your lecture are the most interesting. Say these points in a louder voice. Write them on the board in vibrant colors.

- Repeat what you say several times. This increases the chance that those with fleeting attention will hear it at least once.

- Encourage questions from students. The more actively they are involved in the material being presented, the greater their attention to task.

- Use demonstrations rather than straight lecture. "A picture is worth a thousand words."

Keep the classroom rhythm.

It is critical to consider both ability and attention span when planning lessons. A lively, fast pace is key.

- Keep lessons short. During didactic group instruction, length of attention span is often at its lowest, sometimes limited to five minutes or less. During individualized (one-on-one) instruction attention span usually increases quite a bit and hands-on or experiential learning tasks can capture an ADHD student's attention for much longer. Take note of how

long a particular student can stay on task. Time your lessons accordingly.

- Limit down time during a lesson. ADHD students often have difficulty waiting patiently while teachers are hunting down materials or making last-minute copies. It is at these times that minor disruptions can turn into major disruptions and make it difficult to settle the class down. Have all of your materials organized in advance to reduce teaching lag time. Keep your lesson very well-organized. Write an outline of your lesson on the board or use an overhead projector with transparencies (prepared ahead of time) of the lesson outline. Stick to your outline.

- Limit down time between lessons and periods. Transitions are notoriously difficult for ADHD students. Teachers can easily spend up to a quarter of class time managing transitions between activities. To minimize transition time, it is best to make rules and consequences for transition clear (e.g., follow teacher directions, move quietly, keep hands and feet to yourself). Give clear signals as to the beginning and ending of a period and also give warnings for transition from one activity to another. Rather than say, "It's time to stop working," say: "One more minute to finish the problems, then it will be time to stop." Engage students in activities while they wait for the others to finish transitioning (e.g., have younger students imitate your hand-clapping rhythm, talk to older students about interesting current events)

Involving Peers in the Learning Process

Peer-mediated approaches, such as peer tutoring and cooperative learning, can be particularly effective for teaching ADHD students since these approaches encourage students to be actively involved in the learning process. Their involvement heightens their attention to and interest in the task, and facilitates a high state of learning readiness.

Peer Tutoring: Classwide peer tutoring programs have been developed where all students are paired for tutoring with a classmate (see DuPaul & Stoner, 1994). Students are first given training in the rules and procedures for tutoring their peers in one of a number of subjects such as reading, math,

or spelling. Then, during actual peer tutoring sessions, the tutor reads a script of problems to the tutee and awards points to the tutee for correct responses. Afterwards, they then switch roles, with the tutee becoming the tutor and the tutor becoming the tutee. During these tutoring periods (which are about 20 minutes in length), the teacher walks around the class to make sure the program is being implemented properly and to provide assistance, if needed. Bonus points can be awarded by the teacher to pairs who are following all of the rules. As an incentive, pairs can compete to see who can earn the most points. Peer tutoring is probably most effective for ADHD students when they are paired with well-behaved and conscientious classmates.

Many teachers use peer tutors called "Study Buddies" specifically to help ADHD students develop better study and organizational skills. The buddy helps the ADHD student to do things such as write down assignments, get homework in the backpack, and keep the desk area organized. To avoid social stigma, you may wish to pair all students in your class (with selective pairings of orga-nized with less organized students). Then, instruct pairs to work together and help each other with organizational tasks. It is also a good idea to set up occasions for ADHD students to be in the position of helping their classmates in areas of strength for them (e.g., putting together  a project, reviewing math facts, practicing sports skills, reading to younger students). The tutoring role can be a great self-esteem booster.

Peer Monitoring: Having students monitor their peers' behavior can actually bolster areas of weakness for the student doing the monitoring. For example, one teacher finds that having a child who interrupts a lot keep track of those who are raising their hands greatly reduces the student's inter-ruptions. With training and supervision, students can also learn to monitor

peers' behavior at times like recess, when adult supervisors are in shorter supply. Watch out for peer pressure and rejection though, and never have children administer punishment programs.

Cooperative Learning: A very powerful way to involve peers in the learning process is through cooperative learning groups. Keep in mind, however, that cooperative learning requires that children work together in a manner in which all make contributions and all can get along. Many ADHD students have a lot of trouble working in groups with other children. They may dominate the group or annoy their peers with silly, inappropriate behavior. They may unintentionally hurt the feelings of group members by making fun of their contributions. With ADHD students (and others) cooperation needs to be taught. Start with very small groups (i.e., pairs) and, as with peer tutoring, make a point of pairing ADHD children with compatible peers. You might try assigning specific jobs to each student (e.g.: someone to write down contributions of group members; someone who gets needed materials for the group; someone who calls on group members for contributions). Set rules for the groups such as: everyone needs to participate and support each other. Have students role-play examples of following the rules and not following the rules. Then, during the cooperative learning period, walk from group to group and monitor the students. At the end of the group, have kids evaluate how well their groups worked (what did we do well?, what can we do better next time?). As students are successful working in pairs, you can increase the size of the groups to three or four children.

Promoting Peer Support: Peers often form opinions about their classmates based on how the teacher interacts with the child. All too often, this means that children form judgments about their ADHD classmates in the context of having seen the student reprimanded regularly for negative behavior. Set the stage for peer acceptance and support of the ADHD child. Change the focus to one of supporting the ADHD students and all students when they are doing well. Teach the children to support one another. Use group cheers

for good work or behavior. Reinforce compliments. With your help, peers can be wonderful motivators for success.

Curricula Formats Designed for Enhanced Learning

One of the most powerful predictors of behavior in the classroom is the interest value of the curriculum. ADHD students are drawn to creative, novel, and captivating presentation formats. The extent to which you can design curriculum to include these elements will greatly enhance your success with ADHD (and all) students. Remember to be flexible. Take advantage of as many teachable moments as you can.

Interesting curricula means:

- Using multi-sensory approaches. Present concepts visually, auditorally, and kinesthetically. Kids often remember concepts best when they are presented in many different ways. Have students read about it, hear about it, and act it out.

- Using manipulatives rather than paper-and-pencil tasks. Teach math facts using games and coins. Have them learn measurement skills by building something. Keep a stock of art supplies (e.g., clay, paints, markers) on hand for this purpose.

- Emphasizing experiential learning and individualized projects in areas of interest and strength. Mr. Jay Teeman teaches fifth grade at Roscomare Road Elementary School in Los Angeles, California. He has his fifth grade students select something they know how to do and teach it to the rest of the class. He gives students a list of things they can explain such as making something to eat, a magic trick, a craft, how to play a sport, putting designs on tee shirts. Students pick an activity and briefly explain the process using visual aides. Mr. Daniel Flynn teaches a variety of skills through his "life-skills" unit. Students learn to keep checkbooks, decide on careers, make major purchases, find apartments, read want ads, and learn the pros and cons of many other real life activities (going to the gym, having a pet, tak-

ing out a loan, buying insurance). Math, reading, social studies, and science are all incorporated into this unit, which the students really enjoy.

- Using high interest material. Of course, interesting subject matter is critical. However, just a little spice sprinkled into somewhat dull material can add a spark of interest. Use games during lessons. Use colored sheets of paper, colored chalk. Underline in colors. Use handouts that are presented in a visually interesting way.

- Minimizing rote memorization.

- Using computerized learning programs with self-correction built in. ADHD student's attention is captured by interesting, interactive computer programs in a way that is often hard to duplicate in class.

- Being enthusiastic yourself about the curricula!

Written Assignments and Seatwork

Written work is often the weakest academic area for the ADHD student. Fine motor problems, poor planning of motor responses, and difficulty shifting attention from one activity to another make tasks such as copying, note taking, and giving written responses to readings a real challenge. Attention span is particularly important to consider when planning written assignments. Lengthy, repetitive work is usually difficult for the ADHD student. It requires much more effort on the part of an ADHD student to sustain the attention necessary to complete repetitive work than other students. When faced with columns of math problems or lengthy reading assignments followed by a barrage of questions, ADHD students often give up. If they do attempt the task, they often take much longer to complete the work due to frequent lapses of attention.

To better sustain effort over time and motivate work completion consider the following:

1. Break one large task down into several components. For example, instead of giving the student a big packet of work to complete for the day or week,

give the student one page at a time. Mary Olvak, second grade teacher at P.S. 182, Bronx, NY, uses a checklist to help students complete their work. She breaks up assignments into small steps and each student receives a list of the steps on a sheet of paper. As each step is completed, the student checks it off on the sheet. When the assignment is done, the student signs the bottom of the sheet and turns it in along with the assignment.

2. Limit the amount of work (e.g., problems) on each page to only a few problems or activities so it doesn't seem so overwhelming and cluttered. Cover up portions of the page not being used.

3. Use worksheets that are clearly typed in large bold print.

4. Allot extra time to complete assignments and tests. The extra time enables students to demonstrate their knowledge without being penalized for attention lapses or their difficulty sustaining effort during complex learning tasks.

5. Use a timer. Give students challenges to complete their independent seatwork in a certain period of time. Many students are motivated to "beat the clock"—and, as a result, are better able to sustain their attention to get through a task. Ms. Fran Martin also likes to use the timer for kids who rush through their work. She sets a minimum amount of time to work on a task in order to slow them down!

6. Give work breaks. Paying attention for long periods of time is very effortful and tiring for ADHD students. Work breaks which allow physical movement (e.g., stretching, standing, running an errand) may help some students become more efficient when they are working.

7. Allow students to type their reports on a word processor, or tape record lessons. Use of such strategies enables students to focus their learning effort on subject content rather than getting caught up in details not necessarily relevant to the task at hand.

8. If you can, correct student's work as they do it. Mr. Agler finds this

practice very effective for his ADHD kindergarten and first grade students. He ensures 100% accuracy and completeness by having students correct mistakes before they go on to the next activity. If you find it too time-consuming to check everyone's work, just check the students who need the extra help. Another alternative Mr. Flynn uses is to have daily spot checks for work completion and weekly checks for accuracy. In general, students will learn much more if you give them feedback about their work as soon as they finish it.

9. Reduce the length of the written assignment to match student's attention span. For example, have students complete every other math problem, or require fewer copies of spelling words.

If you do choose to reduce the assignment, make sure the students' understanding of the material is not compromised by their doing less work. Only reduce repetitive or practice work after the concept has been mastered. But, even then, be careful. Some students may be more motivated and successful with shortened assignments, but others may come to expect less from themselves if they are given much shorter assignments. Their self-esteem may suffer if they don't think they can accomplish what their classmates can. Therefore, it is wise to focus your efforts on teaching the students to complete as much work as they can by using strategies such as increased incentives and positive feedback.

Tests
ADHD students often have difficulty taking tests. They may learn the material, but have a hard time reproducing it on an exam. To address this problem, teach your students test-taking strategies. Try the following:

1. Use study sheets completed during class lecture or independent work period and checked by you for accuracy. Study sheets may be fill-in-the-blank, short answer, matching words to definitions, etc. and are to be used as guides for studying for tests.

2. Model frequent underlining and highlighting of main points.

3. Help them make up flash cards for each concept/idea, etc. Play memory games with the flash cards.

4. Show them tricks to remember facts. For visual learners, have them tie concepts with mental images. For verbal learners, have them tie concepts with mnemonics.

5. Give practice tests.

6. Allow students to take tests in a quiet, low distraction area (e.g., cubicle).

7. Allow use of multiple modalities to test knowledge. The written modality is most widely used, but also the area of greatest challenge for many ADHD children. Consider allowing oral presentations and projects to test knowledge. Often, this is where ADHD students can shine! Make it more interesting by letting kids use a microphone when they give an oral report.

8. Give extra time, if needed.

Long-term Reports
ADHD students are notorious procrastinators. Assigning a book report that's due a month away will be a problem for most ADHD students. They are attracted to immediate rewards. That means the book report does not become important until the day before it is due. To circumvent this tendency, they will need to know how to break up large assignments into doable parts and they will need to be rewarded for completing each part, not just for the finished product. Mr. Flynn has developed a method for teaching students to complete book reports that does just that. He divides the report into sections which are completed one at a time over the course of several weeks. For example, the students in Mr. Flynn's class complete a "Countries of the World Report." Each student selects a country and then writes a report about it. The report is divided into three sections: the History

Section, the Government Section, and the Opinion Section. The student completes a data/fact collection sheet for each section. This sheet carefully guides the student through the process of collecting specific information and summarizing it into paragraphs. This is the data/fact collection sheet for the History Section of the report:

History Section Assignmnent:

Using at least two paragraphs, describe the history of the country.

Paragraph one:
Past history: Describe the history of the country. Be sure to include the native people or tribes of the country, when the current government was founded, the event or circumstances that formed the current government, and one famous leader.

Paragraph two:
Recent history: Give a description of the recent history of your country. Be sure to include what your country did during World War II, any wars or uprisings since the year you were born, and at least one important person from your country and why he/she is important.

This level of detail gives the student plenty of structure to be thorough and specific.

Mr. Flynn finds it important to enlist parent support in helping children complete the report. He gives the following information to parents about how they can best assist their children with the report:

Tips for Helping with Long-Term Reports	
DO	**DON'T**
Encourage your child to start report early enough to complete assignment in time	Be unaware of your child's time line
Assist your child in where to find resources (i.e., card catalog, librarian, computer, etc.) in the library	Find the resources for your child
Make yourself available early enough in the process	Reinforce your child's procrastination by allowing yourself to bail him or her out at the last minute
Encourage and assist your child to organize information logically	Organize and rewrite information for your child
Type your child's final report identically from your child's re-written handwritten rough draft	Make corrections/revisions while typing your child's final report
Tell your child to look it up in the dictionary when he or she wants to know how a word is spelled	Tell your child how to spell an unknown or misspelled word
Have your child assist in the whole final report process	Do the report for your child

As each data/fact collection sheet is complete, the student goes on to the next. After all section data/fact collection sheets are complete and checked by the teacher, the student simply compiles the information gathered from the sheets onto a rough draft worksheet. After the rough draft is corrected by the teacher, the final report is written. Using this system, ADHD students have been successful in finishing lengthy, detailed book reports on time!

Homework

Homework is usually a struggle for families of ADHD children. Work that takes some students 30 minutes to do may take an ADHD student over an hour. Lengthy homework often leads to heated family arguments and becomes demoralizing for ADHD students. Don't set families up; be realistic in the amount of work assigned for homework. Don't send incomplete classwork home as homework. If a student doesn't complete work in class, it's unlikely that it will be done with much success at home either (unless the parent does it). For kindergarten and first graders, 10 minutes of homework per night is plenty (if any is assigned at all). For second and third grade, 30 minutes should be the limit. For fourth through sixth grade, one or two 30 minute blocks of homework per night is probably sufficient. Remember that it usually takes much longer for ADHD students to complete their work (especially if it is written).

- Communicate your expectations about homework.
  At the beginning of the year, be clear with parents and students about what your expectations are for homework. What are your goals for homework? Should parents help the student? How much? What kind of homework will be assigned each night? Is it meant as practice for skills taught in class, or does it have some other purpose? How long should it take? To help make homework expectations explicit, Ms. Donna Hall, a third grade teacher at Culverdale Elementary School in Irvine, California, distributes the following homework contract to all families at the beginning of each school year:

Dear Parents:

In order to insure that all persons concerned will understand my policy for homework, I would like you to discuss the following contract with your child and then have both of you sign it. I have previously reviewed this with your child in class. If you have any questions, please contact me or have your child see me at school.

As the teacher, I will provide:
1. instructional background for the work.
2. materials needed in student mailboxes.
3. reminder of the work on the homework chart.

Teacher's signature

As the parent, I will:
1. provide a quiet work area.
2. provide a designated time for homework.
3. monitor work as needed (watch neatness).
4. show pleasure over completed work and initial the work.
5. write a note to my teacher if the child was confused about the assignment.

Parent's signature

As the student, I will:
1. try my very best on my own.
2. use my neatest handwriting.
3. turn my work in on time.
4. have my parent initial my finished work.
5. let my teacher know if I had any problems.
6. show all my school work to my parents each night.
7. have my parents sign any important papers and return them to school.

Student's signature

Ms. Hall adds a bonus for students who complete homework assignments. At the bottom of this contract she states that: "Completed work will be rewarded on the last Friday of the month. Students who have missed no more than four assignments will qualify for the special movie. Those who do not qualify will work on independent work."

● Use homework assignment sheets.

When you give assignments, be as clear as you possibly can. Write down the homework assignment each day in class and make a point to go over the assignment thoroughly. Have students repeat back the assignment to make sure they understand. Students should also keep track of the homework on a homework assignment sheet (like the sample below). The student writes down the assignment as well as the materials needed and due date. The teacher checks to make sure the assignment is written correctly and signs the form. The parent can also sign the form after the assigned homework is completed. A weekly assignment sheet listing assignments for each day of the week can be used. Alternatively, you may prefer to use a daily assignment sheet with each subject or period listed separately (for example, subjects can be listed in place of days on the sample form). Long and short-term assignments can also be listed separately.

Homework Assignment Sheet

Week of:	Assignment	Books and materials needed	Due date	Teacher's signature	Parent's signature
Monday					
Tuesday					
Wednesday					
Thursday					
Friday					

Be sure not to neglect the importance of checking students' completed homework and providing students feedback as soon as possible! If feedback is very delayed (or does not occur at all), students may end up not taking homework very seriously.

- Help parents encourage homework completion.
  Many parents have difficulty getting their children to do homework and would benefit from your suggestions. First of all, emphasize the importance of their staying informed about the homework assignments. They should be encouraged to check to make sure the assignment sheet is complete and signed by the teacher each day and that the proper materials have been brought home. Let parents know that having a set time and place to do the work is usually a good idea. The time should be selected to fit into the family schedule. You might want to give students the homework well in advance of the due date (give homework due on Friday at the beginning of the week). Parents and students can then choose which nights the student is to complete the homework so that planned family activities and sports don't have to be sacrificed. The place to do homework should be one in which the child feels comfortable and not overly distracted. Tell parents to allow their children to have short work breaks (often a necessity for ADHD children since they have trouble focusing their attention for long). Encourage parents to monitor and check their child's work (but not do the work for him or her). Parents should also make a point to reward their children for getting the work done. You might want to give parents suggestions about rewards to use based on what you see works in class (e.g., praise, certain activities, stickers, chore passes). Since productivity is usually the problem, tell parents to set up rewards for the amount and accuracy of work completed, not just simply looking like they are doing it. Sometimes it's also helpful for the parent to serve as a good role model and schedule to work on some "homework-like" tasks during the time the child is working on homework. *Most importantly:* Advise parents that homework can easily fall through the cracks if parents aren't involved.

Interventions for Behavior in the Parallel Teaching Model

The final part of parallel teaching involves using interventions to manage attention and behavior. Since good attention and behavior are prerequisites to learning, interventions are considered to be an integral part of the teaching process. Basic interventions include: scanning the classroom, having students participate and stay involved, setting rules, giving clear directions, and using strategic praise and prudent corrective feedback.

The parallel teaching style considers these interventions as a spice to be sprinkled liberally throughout the lesson. Whether behavior is good or bad, attentive or off-task, the teacher using this style will insert frequent interventions while simultaneously delivering the lesson plan. These interventions are intended for use with the entire class, with more frequent use necessary for ADHD students. Using "interventions" may feel like an annoying interruption of your lesson plan; yet, without them, good behavior goes unnoticed and negative behavior often escalates until it must be noticed. By that time, the behavior is more out-of-control and you will likely feel frustrated about having to stop teaching in order to reprimand students who are off-task.

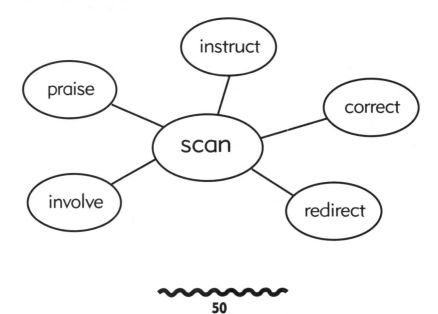

Here is an example of how one teacher uses parallel teaching. Look for the basic elements: scanning, involving students, setting rules, giving clear directions, using strategic praise and corrective feedback.

Teacher: Let's review the stages of life of the butterfly. Can anyone tell me what they are? Teacher scans class with careful attention to Bill, a student who has ADHD. She notices that Bill is not paying attention. She decides to involve Bill at this point so that he is more likely to tune in for the rest of the discussion.

Teacher: Bill, (waits briefly until he gives her eye contact, a sign that he is paying attention) can you tell me the stages of life of the butterfly? (involves student, gives clear directions)

Bill: First there is an egg, then the egg turns into a caterpillar, then it spins into a pupa, then it turns into a butterfly.

Teacher: That's right. You remembered all four stages. I like the way you listened to the question and gave me good eye contact. That way I know that you are listening. (strategic praise in a pleasant, non-accusatory voice tone).

In this example, the teacher could have chosen not to repeat the question, but instead have asked Bill the answer or reprimanded him for not listening. If either of these two options were selected, the teacher might have missed the opportunity to praise Bill for attending successfully. The ADHD student has had many years of being scolded for his misbehavior. By the time you have such children in your class, they may feel that they can't be successful. Your job is to teach them that they can be successful.

Let's look at another example:

Teacher: (While talking about government in Texas, the teacher scans the class every minute or so to see if everyone is attending. During a scan, she notices that Sui is trying to show his neighbor, Justin, a toy from home.

Justin has not yet directed his attention to Sui . She walks over to Sui , who fortunately is sitting near her and says): I like the way Justin is paying close attention. (strategic praise) Justin, can you tell me the capital of Texas? (While talking, she opens her hand to Sui without saying a word. Sui puts the toy in her hand).

Justin: Austin.

Teacher: (still standing next to Sui) Good listening, Justin. (strategic praise) Sui, no toys during class. I need your eyes and ears on me. (prudent corrective feedback, lesson continues)

Here, the teacher could have told Sui to put the toy away from across the room and scolded him for playing. She also could have waited a few seconds to see if Justin would respond. The timing on this intervention was critical. She stopped the problem because she caught it very early. It helped having the "high-risk" child right by her so she could watch his every move. She also minimized what she said to Sui, saving him from public embarrassment. Removing the toy prevented future disruptions.

Let's see how to use this model to handle calling out, a pervasive problem among ADHD students.

Teacher: Let's do some long division problems together. Before we get started, can someone tell me what rule everyone should follow during this time? (sets rule with student input)

Bill: You have to raise your hand to talk.

Teacher: That's right. The handraising rule is in effect. OK, here's the problem: What is 968 divided by 4?" (Teacher writes the problem on the board.) "What's the first step? (involves student)

Lisa calls out the correct answer without raising her hand. Teacher surveys the classroom and notices that two other students have raised their hands and remained silent. (scans)

Teacher: Lisa, that's an interruption. (prudent corrective feedback) I liked the way Miguel and Susan remembered to raise their hands. (strategic praise) Miguel, what's the first step? (involves student)

In this example, the teacher correctly enforced the handraising rule by using interventions while teaching. This usually takes active attention to the class process. It is often tempting to respond to the student who calls out, especially if the answer is correct, and accept it. However, this means that the handraising rule is not enforced. In effect, the students who follow this rule end up being punished and the students who violate the rule are reinforced. The result is that students learn not to take the class rules seriously. Remember, ADHD students may be particularly susceptible to this negative learning process. Here again, your role as a teacher involves not only teaching academic concepts, but also teaching students how to follow rules and directions.

Guidelines for Using Interventions in Parallel Teaching

To use these interventions effectively, think "in parallel." Develop the habit of thinking about the lesson plan and behavior simultaneously, weaving smoothly from teaching to intervention and back to teaching. As illustrated above, interventions should be brief (two seconds). Emphasize positive behaviors ("I see Cornell working;" "I like the way Sherri is listening;" "Looks like the entire first row is paying attention;" etc.) and involve students in the lesson ("Tasha, tell me what punctuation mark goes at the end of this sentence?" "Mark, what is the answer to this math problem?") Other interventions, such as setting rules and giving clear directions ("Everyone, get your math book and open to page 25"), should be used to promote compliance and prevent problem behavior. Corrective feedback (e.g., "That's an interruption;" "That's minus one point for not following directions;") should be used to stop disruptive behavior.

Timing of interventions is critical since you want to catch good behavior before it stops and stop negative behavior before it gets out of hand. On average, set your mental clock for about one or two minutes. Scan your

classroom at this interval looking for a student (especially the ADHD student) who is attending or on-task and provide a brief intervention that involves the student or gives positive attention. During your scan, you should also keep your eyes open for students who are inattentive or silently daydreaming. Give them interventions that involve or redirect them. Students who are being disruptive should receive immediate corrective feedback. If behavior is mostly positive, you will probably need to give only one or two interventions per scan. If behavior is very problematic, you may need to take more time during your scan so that you can provide interventions to more students. During each scan, you should try to make at least one of your interventions either positive attention or one that involves a student (or students) in the lesson. Remember that asking students questions or having students participate in the lesson in some way is considered an intervention because it helps students maintain attention to the task.

If you teach a lower grade or have many behavior problems in your class, you may need to scan the class more frequently than the one to two minute guideline so that you can be sure to catch good behavior when it happens. On the other hand, if you have few behavior problems or you teach a higher grade, you should be able to lengthen this interval. Likewise, you should vary this approach for different activities and class periods. During high-interest or hands-on activities, frequent interventions may be unnecessary to maintain attention to task. During times when ADHD students are prone to having difficulty staying on-task, such as during independent seatwork, lengthy lessons, or transitions, frequent interventions may be critical. Keep in mind that when most of the class is working during independent seatwork, interventions that the entire class can hear may break some students' concentration. In this case, it is better to move close to the off-task student and give a brief redirection in a low tone of voice. Note that since you can't assume perfect behavior equals perfect attending, you shouldn't stop your interventions altogether even if you don't have behavior problems.

When you are first learning this approach, you may find it hard to scan every one or two minutes. You might be more successful if you start with less frequent scans until you get the hang of it. You should also plan and practice giving these interventions. Before or after class, plan what behavior you want to attend to, how you can involve students, and what directions and corrective statements you may need to make. Then, practice giving the interventions. With planning and practice, these sorts of interventions should become much easier, even automatic. The following describes how to use each of the basic types of interventions:

Setting Rules

Having clear rules helps set the stage for all other interventions. While ADHD students may understand class rules, they don't adjust their behavior to conform to the rules. They react in the moment and often forget the rules unless they are made very clear and salient.

Guidelines for Establishing Rules

Involve the students in generating the rules. On the first day of class, make a list of 4-5 rules using suggestions from students. Word rules in a clear, positive way. Wording in a positive way keeps students' attention focused on what they are to do, instead of what they are not to do. Here are some examples:

> ① Keep hands and feet to yourself
>
> ② Follow teacher's directions
>
> ③ Respect people's feelings and their property
>
> ④ Listen with your body

Other rules you could include are: Use quiet voices in the classroom, Walk in the classroom and in the school, Use good manners, and Line up quietly.

Write rules in large bold lettering on a large piece of construction paper. If you like, add pictures depicting each rule (especially with younger children). Assign each rule a number or color for easy reference later. Make sure students understand each rule. Have students give examples of rule-following behavior as well as rule violations. Post rules in a place easily seen by all students in class.

Guidelines for Implementing Rules

Simply establishing the rules will not guarantee that they will be followed. It is essential to prompt rule following. You can do this by reviewing the rules every day, and especially before each activity (after a couple of weeks this can be faded). Have selected students give examples of following the rules. Then, throughout the day, you can have "rule checks" inserted while you teach. Praise individual students who are following one or more of the rules. It is especially important to notice when ADHD students are following the rules, since they benefit from frequent feedback about their behavior. Here are some examples:

"It's time for a rule check. I see Corinne is following rule #5 and Ben is following rule #2. I see the entire first row has rule #3 perfected!"

"Hold on to that question and keep raising your hand, Nancy. I'll get to you in a minute."

If you notice one student not following a rule, point out those who are. This often motivates the student to follow the rule without ever having to give direct negative attention to the behavior. Be sure to comment on that child's behavior once it is "in line" with the rules.

Use hand signals and other visual prompts. Kids often respond better to nonverbal prompts as opposed to verbal reminders (especially lengthy verbal reminders). Have a signal for each rule. For example, if rules are numbered

you can raise the number of fingers corresponding to the specific rule followed. Other examples include: raising fingers to your lips to signal quiet, raising palm to signal stop, shaking head to signal no. Mr. Agler uses a voice meter in his kindergarten-first grade class to teach appropriate voice volume. The voice meter has settings for No Talking, Whisper Voice, Classroom Voice or Inside Voice, Playground Voice, or Outside Voice. He sets the voice meter before each activity for all students to see. Students are praised for keeping their voices within the selected level. If an individual student or the class becomes too loud, the voice meter serves as a reminder. Be consis-

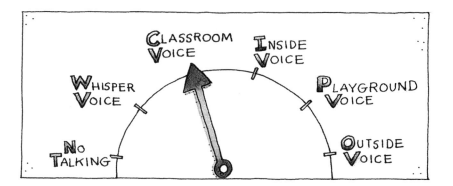

tent in enforcing the rules. Letting a child "get away" with rule violations even one time makes it harder for the student to follow the rule next time.

Involving Students in Lessons

One of the most beneficial things you can do to prevent problems and maximize learning is to INVOLVE the ADHD student. These kids thrive on interaction, and involvement in the lesson will make the difference between engagement and disengagement. Involving the students (especially those with ADHD) should be an ongoing part of your teaching. Have ADHD students become involved right away in your lesson. Then, continue to involve them as they attend to the lesson or if you sense that they may start drifting off or becoming disruptive.

Use these strategies to involve students:

- Check to see that the student is following along on the right page or giving you eye contact when appropriate. Use physical prompts as necessary (point to the right page, move student's chair into the proper position).

- Ask questions. Call on the ADHD student ("Who can tell me...?") or have the students respond in unison. Routinely check students' understanding of the lecture. Keep in mind that ADHD students often require more time to respond to questions.

- Encourage active responses during lessons. Have students solve problems at the blackboard, use physical movement to signal answers (e.g., thumbs up means yes, thumbs down means no). Have them play-act answers. Give students activity sheets to complete mid-point in a lesson or at the end. Vary the pattern.

- Have the ADHD student be a teacher's assistant during lessons and during transitions. Allow the student to turn pages, use a pointer, or get materials needed for your lecture or demonstration. Use the student's worksheet as an example for the class.

Giving Directions

Directions may be given as a way to instruct during a lesson or as a way to manage behavior. Unfortunately, ADHD students' short attention span, lack of inhibition, and distractibility all interfere with their compliance. To increase the likelihood that ADHD students will listen and follow your directions, use these guidelines:

Guidelines for Giving Instructions to Individual Students

1. Get student's attention, preferably with eye contact, before giving directions. Use standard phrase or sign: "Stop, Look, and Listen."

2. Stand close to the student. Don't yell from across the room. This requirement is eased by having the students with the most difficulty following

directions be seated close to you.

3. Be specific about what you want the child to do.

4. Be brief.

5. Make a statement; don't ask a question. Precede your direction with: "You have a direction to...(e.g., go to your seat, get your book out, follow the quiet rule)."

6. When appropriate, give choices: "You have a math page and a science page to complete. Which would you like to do first?" "You can choose to continue drawing now or you can choose to clean-up now. If you choose to clean-up, you'll earn your recess. If not, you will have to sit out of the recess game and you will still need to clean up."

7. Have the student repeat back the instruction to ensure understanding (e.g., "What are your instructions?"). One teacher with over 30 students in her class found this to be the most important part about giving directions to her ADHD students.

See the chart on page 60 for specific problems.

Guidelines for Giving Directions to Groups

1. Make sure everyone is quiet and is giving you eye contact.

2. Walk around the room to be sure students' attention is not compromised by fiddling with toys or writing notes to friends.

3. Keep the directions simple.

4. Use visual cues along with verbal directions. Write instructions on the board, or an overhead.

5. Walk students through the directions.

6. Ask for unison responses to repeat the direction.

7. Quiz students regarding the directions to ensure understanding.

Do's and Don'ts for Giving Effective Directions

Statement	Problem	Better
"Jason, would you collect all of the papers?"	Implies a choice.	"Jason, please collect the papers."
"Okay, class. It's time to get back to work. Turn to chapter 5 of your book and you will find an experiment to do. All of the materials are on the back counter. Make sure to answer all questions on the worksheet. When you're done, turn in your worksheet. Then it will be time to start your math."	Too many directions at once.	Give time, such as 5-10 seconds, in between each direction.
"I need everyone to show good behavior."	Too vague.	Define good behavior, "I need everyone to sit properly, hands on desk, and show me your eyes. That way I know you are listening."
"Pleeeze! Be quiet!!!!!"	Too emotional.	Stay calm. Use a nonverbal sign—turn off the lights, use a hand signal—to tell students its time to be quiet.
"Why can't you ever listen the first time?"	Unanswerable question.	Be direct. "You have a direction to listen the first time."
"Put all of your things in your desk."	The direction would work for most students, but is too general for ADHD students.	Give more specific directions and help the students organize where their things should go.
"Do you want to lose your recess?	A threat given in an emotional way can provoke many ADHD students	"If you don't finish your work, you will lose your recess."

Using your Attention Strategically

Using positive attention strategically is one of the most important interventions in parallel teaching. It means that you purposely use your positive attention to help students remain on task and redirect those who aren't. When using positive attention strategically, you search for and attend to positive behaviors throughout the day (especially those you want to see more of). For ADHD students, this means *you may need to attend to behaviors that you ordinarily expect students to do without difficulty such as getting started on assigned work, raising a hand to talk, or staying seated properly during a class discussion.* Remember that ADHD students typically enjoy words of encouragement and praise. They seem to need more frequent positive feedback than other students. Walking around the room and touching the students' shoulder or back while they are working is a very helpful way to keep them on-task. When minor behavior problems do occur, attend to and praise those students who are on-task and ignore the off-task student. That student is likely to copy or model those students who were praised in an attempt to gain your attention as well. Remember to praise immediately once the problem student is back on task. To get the most from your praise, pay close attention to the "high risk" situations for ADHD students (individual seatwork, long repetitive lessons, transitions between activities, unstructured times). Give extra praise at these times. See the chart on the next page for tips about giving praise.

While ignoring is useful for some mild misbehaviors, immediate corrective feedback is required for more disruptive behavior. Your corrective feedback needs to be just as strategic as your positive feedback. Negative teacher attention can be reinforcing, and perpetuate the problem you are trying to correct. To use corrective feedback strategically, keep it immediate and brief. It is only one tool in the context of an otherwise positive, engaging instructional program.

Keep in mind that positive behavior may not always present itself to you as dramatically as negative behavior. This makes it harder to keep up your rates

Tips for Praising

Be specific. Label the behavior you like.

Say: "I like the way you followed directions right away," not just "thank you."

Say: "You have done a great job completing all of those problems," not just "good job."

Praise immediately when you see positive behavior. If you wait, you may miss your chance or you may forget.

Praise improvement. Don't wait for heroic efforts or an "A" paper. ADHD students often benefit from praise for acts that other students do automatically. Notice the little things which are big things for ADHD students:

You got your pencil and book out right away! You found the right page!

You're being patient! You remembered to raise your hand! I noticed you completed that tough division problem.

Keep your praise free from put-downs and instructions, no matter how subtle.

Don't say: You should always keep your desk that clean.

Say: Your desk is spotless!

Don't say: Finally, you remembered your homework.

Say: I like the way you remembered your homework today.

Be genuine and enthusiastic. Don't count on perfunctory praise. Take the extra effort to walk over to the student and show your pleasure at his or her behavior. Make it a practice to publicly announce good effort and accomplishments. But, if you sense a particular student might be embarrassed by such attention, do it privately.

Praise often. ADHD students need to hear positive feedback often. Try to set a goal of giving five to ten praises every hour. Even more important, keep the ratio of positive to negative feedback high. While you should make a point to praise ADHD students regularly, you also don't want to forget about your other students.

of praise and you may end up inter-acting with students only when problems occur. To avoid this, you may need to give yourself reminders to praise more often. Some teachers find that posting a reminder sign (e.g., "Catch Them Being Good") in an area they are liable to look helps. Whenever they look at the sign they are reminded to praise. Some teachers like to keep track of their rates of praise. You might use a tally sheet for this. Another method is to store tokens in a clothing pocket. Each time you praise, move a token from one pocket to another. Set a goal of transferring all of the tokens by the end of the period or day.

Don't expect that ADHD stu-dents will change dramatically with the use of praise and ignoring. ADHD students typically need rich-er incentives to motivate positive behavior.

Setting Limits

Choose your battles. If you com-mented on every instance of off-task behavior in your classroom, you would have little time left for instruction. Choose your battles

---

Tips for Ignoring

Only ignore behavior that is intended for your attention. Ignoring works well for whining, argu-ing, repeated complaints about the fairness of an established rule, and low level non-disruptive misbehavior. Ignoring also works well for students who call out answers in class and blurt out of turn. If the goal of a stu-dent's behavior is to get out of work-ing or following a direction or is intended to gain the attention of peers, ignoring won't work.

Use active ignoring, when you choose to ignore. Purposely ignore misbehavior by not comment-ing on it and not looking at the stu-dent. Be consistent. Problems will increase if you ignore the behavior sometimes and then attend to it at other times. Warning: Ignored behav-ior may initially get worse. Have a plan to deal with this.

Stop ignoring the moment you see the student start behaving properly. Praise the good behavior immediately.

Never ignore aggressive or destructive behavior. Use strate-gies for setting limits discussed below. Time-out or a loss of privi-leges may be necessary.

strategically. Corrective feedback is generally not necessary for brief, non-disruptive off-task behavior. Prioritize those behaviors which may require correction. For example which is more important: having the student stay seated during the entire lesson, or remembering to raise his hand before speaking? Pick one area to focus on. Once you have success in one area, you can go onto the next.

Use prudent corrective feedback. The importance of using a prudent approach when correcting hyperactive students has been driven home in a series of research studies conducted by Dr. Susan O'Leary and her colleagues at the State University of New York at Stony Brook (Abramowitz & O'Leary, 1991, Pfiffner & O'Leary, 1993). Prudent approaches stop problem behavior in its tracks; imprudent approaches can escalate problems to all new heights. What is a prudent approach? It involves giving corrective or negative feedback in a brief, specific, and direct way. The feedback is given right after the negative behavior starts and every time the negative behavior occurs. It is also given in close proximity to the student and in a calm, matter-of-fact tone of voice. See the chart on this page for specific examples.

Prudent and Imprudent Feedback

Prudent	Imprudent
Brian, please get to work.	Brian, why aren't you working?!
Stop talking or you will have to go back to your seat.	How many times do I have to tell you to stop talking? Other students can't concentrate when you are so loud. You know the quiet rule. You're going to have to learn how to follow it.
I gave you a direction to clean up. If you don't start right away, you will start losing recess time.	I told you before recess to clean up your mess. I noticed that you went to recess anyway. You have to remember to clean up before recess.

For persistent or more serious problems, loss of privileges, tokens, work tasks or time-out become necessary. The prudent use of these consequences will be discussed on page 116.

Specialized Curricula for ADHD Students
Organizational and Study Skills

A common and very frustrating experience for ADHD students, their teachers, and parents is to find that work was completed, only it was the wrong assignment.
Organizational and study skills need to be taught to ADHD students. Fortunately, there are many tricks to help improve these skills. Try the following:

a) Use one 3-ring notebook with a pouch containing lots of pencils and erasers and dividers for each subject. The notebook should include a:

- homework assignment page (see page 48). You can also add a column for in-class assignments.

- pocket folder to hold papers/tests until they are punched (it's better to have all papers punched before giving to student).

- color code for each subject.

- stack of extra paper.

b) Monitor use of the notebook every day. Students can typically learn this system, but without consistent reinforcement, will fail to use it. Have the students write down the following steps on an index card taped inside their notebook and lead them through each one.

> Did I turn in my homework assignment?
>
> Did I write todays class and homework assignment and the due dates in my book?
>
> Did I put away all returned papers and tests in the right place?
>
> Did I put away all handouts and worksheets in the right place?

c) Do periodic desk checks (at least weekly, preferably daily to begin with). Help students organize their belongings and throw out trash. Give rewards for a clean desk and for following directions during the clean-out time.

d) Tape a file folder to the side of each student's desk to store worksheets/assignments with separate sections for complete and incomplete work.

e) Teach notetaking. Use an outline on the board or on a handout. Stick to it. Highlight key points by underlining, using different colors,etc. Tell students the important points to write down. Give students a handout to make sure that they have all the important ideas.

f) Check students' notes. Give points for getting the main ideas. Let students make an appointment with you after school to catch up on their notes. Try assigning study buddies. The buddy can be called upon to check completeness of notes and can help fill in details. But make sure the buddy doesn't end up doing all of the work.

g) Practice time estimation. It is not unusual for ADHD students to believe an assignment will take less time than it actually does. Have them time themselves completing an assignment. They should save the results so that they can more accurately estimate time for completing future projects.

Social Skills

ADHD children are at great risk for being rejected by their peers. Just as teachers and parents find their behavior difficult to tolerate, so do other children. ADHD children tend to be intrusive, impatient, easily frustrated, easily

bored, bossy, self-centered, insensitive to social cues, and not inclined to follow rules. Inattention and lack of concentration make it difficult for them to hold conversations. These characteristics do not win many friends. Yet most ADHD children desperately want friends. Their repeated social failures can be devastating to them.

As a teacher there is much you can do to improve the social behavior of your ADHD students. You can work individually with students in need; however, your entire class is likely to benefit from direct instruction in social skills. A model social skills training program for ADHD elementary-age students has been developed at UCI-CDC (Kotkin, 1995). The most intensive version of the training program is in place at the UCI-CDC day treatment facility, and consists of daily hour-long groups. Less intensive versions are in place at local public schools (occurring twice per week for 12 weeks), and at an after-school program for ADHD youngsters (occurring once per week for eight weeks). The program is implemented as a formal class and teaches a number of specific sportsmanship skills that are often a problem for ADHD youngsters. Students learn the skills and then practice using the skills during games. ADHD youngsters usually have no difficulty learning the skills; their greatest challenge comes in using the skills in "real life" situations. This means that these students require lots of practice and feedback before they are able to use the skills routinely. The following format is based on the program developed at the UCI-CDC:

- **Select an important skill to work on.** Skills that are common problems for ADHD children include: Following game rules, participating and staying with the game, cheering others, cooperating, helping, sharing, tolerating frustration and accepting consequences, being assertive, ignoring provocation, and solving problems. Work on one of these skills at a time. The amount of time spent on each skill will depend on the needs of your class. Changing "target" skills every week or two may best maintain stu-

dent interest. You can always rotate back through skills that need more work after you have covered several others.

- **Introduce the "skill of the week" in an animated and brief didactic fashion.** One of the most valuable aspects to social skills training is developing a common vocabulary to describe the skills. Clearly identify the skill, by saying, for example, "We are working on cooperation."  Then review how, when and why to use it. Actively involve the students (especially the ADHD child) in the discussion. You may want to use a group challenge game to reinforce participation. For example, give tokens (e.g., "good sports bucks") to children who participate in the discussion. If the class earns a certain number of "bucks," they get to pick a game of their choice to play at the end.

- **Model the skill of the week.** You should demonstrate both the right and wrong way (kids usually enjoy seeing their teacher do it the wrong way!).

- **Have the students role-play the positive use of the skill in selected situations.** Give kids brief scripts to follow, such as joining a game, responding to a request to play, leaving a game, and responding to teasing. After each role-play, have students evaluate each other. For example, a thumbs up means the student did a good job and used most of the targeted social skills, a medium thumbs (parallel to the floor) means the student used some of the skills but left out an important one, and a thumbs down means the student didn't use the skill. Students should share why they gave the ratings they did. Focus on the positive as much as possible. Let students redo role-plays that receive poor ratings. You should also be sensitive to ADHD students' feelings of rejection and exercise caution during these evaluations.

- **Have the students participate in a group game to practice the skills.** Use a variety of indoor games (e.g., board games, "rainy day games") and outdoor games (e.g., team sports, circle games). Plan on about a 15-minute game period. Just before the game, have the students predict how well they will do showing good social skills. You may want to use the Goodsport Thermometer described below. Then during the game, give students immediate feedback regarding their use of the skills. You may want to provide tokens for kids showing certain social skills during the group game.

- **When the game is completed, have the students review their performance.** You can have them match their ratings with the teacher evaluation using the Goodsport Thermometer below. Have them tell you what went well and what they could do to make it go even better next time.

- **Reward them for using the skills taught.** This also promotes group cohesion. For example, you could offer a group party (e.g., pizza or popcorn party) when the class meets a specific goal. At the UCI-CDC school, kids earn pizza parties for showing good social skills. A large poster board contains a picture of a pizza with space for a pre-determined number of pepperonis Students earn pepperonis either individually or as a group for showing the "social skill of the day (or week)." Once all of the pepperonis have been earned, the class gets the pizza party. You might also want to reward good behavior and participation during the social skills lesson with either a game at the end of class or extra tokens toward the party.

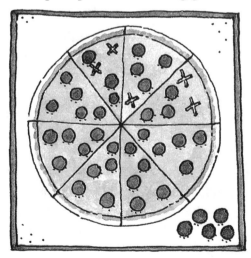

• **At times other than during the social skills lesson, periodically award the class for showing the social skill of the week.** This way you will increase use of the skills across the entire day.

For an individual ADHD student with more severe social deficits, you might also want to institute an individual token economy or school-home report card targeting specific areas of concern for that child. Also, be aware that most ADHD children do not generalize these skills to other settings (e.g., recess, home, after-school programs, team sports) on their own. They need coaching and reinforcement for good social skills in *all* settings. Therefore, it is recommended that you send home a list of the social skills you are working on in class and examples of each skill. That way, parents can reinforce the skills at home and help the child generalize what was learned in class.

Using the Goodsport Thermometer

A "Goodsport Thermometer" is a visual aid developed by the staff at the UCI-CDC school for helping kids set goals and evaluate their own behavior. The Goodsport Thermometer has a five point rating scale to monitor the presence or absence of "good sport" behavior during games. Higher scores mean more good sport behavior. For exceptional good sport behavior by all students, the thermometer goes above a five and "breaks."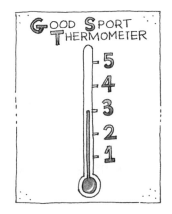

You can use the Goodsport Thermometer in a variety of ways and for a variety of purposes. Try the following: (Agler, 1995)
Prompt students to think about good sport behaviors before the game (e.g., "What do you think we have to do to get a five on the Goodsport Thermometer during freeze tag?"). Have kids predict how well they think they will do right before they start a game.

Make a Good Sport bulletin board displaying the thermometer to monitor students' progress each day. Go over progress with the class (e.g., "When we get a five on the Goodsport Thermometer we mark it on the chart. Look how many fives we have scored!").

After the game is over, have students evaluate how they did and compare their ratings of the game with others (e.g., "I voted for a four for that game. Who matched with me? Why did you vote for a four?"). Use the teacher rating as the "gold standard."

Have students explore the association between good sportsmanship and their feelings during games (e.g., "I noticed that most of you say you had fun on days when the class votes for a five on the Goodsport Thermometer !").

Reward high ratings with group cheers and tokens such as Good Sport Bucks, exchangeable for group rewards. Prompt the positive alternative behaviors when the class earns less than a five (e.g., "What can we do next time to make our soccer game a five?").

Use the thermometer frequently at the beginning of the year (when the skills are first being learned and the class is still developing cohesion). Over time, you can fade its use. This procedure helps students to learn quickly what is expected and rewarded during games and activities.

Here is a sample social skills lesson based on the social skills program at the UCI-CDC:

Lesson topic: Accepting Consequences

Teacher: Today we are going to talk about what you can do when something happens that you don't like or when things don't go your way. Let's say you are mad because someone called you out in a game. You know you should be out but you are mad because you want to keep playing. Now there are a lot of things you can do. You can get really mad and start yelling at the person who called you out (teacher models yelling). You can get so upset that you start crying (teacher models crying). You can go to the coach

and starting whining about it (teacher models whining). All of these might be high risk choices, though. What's wrong with these choices?

Jamal: You can get in trouble for fighting.

Lilly: You can lose friends. People won't want to play with you.

Osiris: You can get kicked out of the game.

Teacher: That's right. They're high risk choices because they might get you in trouble. What would be a better choice?

Ahmad: Just go out.

Teacher: That's a good idea. In our class, that's called accepting. Accepting is when you keep on following the rules and getting along with others when something happens that you don't like or don't want. Let's talk about how you can show accepting. First, how do you think your body should look? Like this (teacher clenches her hands) or like this (teacher models a calm body)?

Osiris: Like the second time.

Teacher: That's right. You can show accepting by having a calm body posture. Arms and hands are by my side. My face is relaxed. Now how should I sound? Like this (teacher loudly says: "It's not fair!! You're cheating!! I don't have to go out if I don't want to!") or this (teacher calmly says: "Darn it, I wish I wasn't out")?

Ahmad: You should be like the second time: Not yelling.

Teacher: That's right. Why do you think it is important to show accepting?

Jamal: You should show accepting because you will have more friends and the game will be more fun.

Teacher: When do you think you should show accepting?

Lilly: You should show accepting when you are called out, or when you

don't get to do something you wanted to do.

Teacher: Those are good answers. Jamal, Lilly, Ahmad, and Osiris all earned participation points for their contributions. So you can show you are accepting by what you look like and what you sound like. You're body should look calm and your voice should be calm. Let's do some role-plays to practice accepting.

(Teacher gives two students a brief script to follow that involves their being called out during a game of tag. They practice for a moment and then the teacher and the students do the role-play in front of the rest of the class.)

Role-play
Teacher: Mark and Susie you were just tagged so you have to go to the sidelines.

Mark: (frowns and sighs, but goes out) OK.

Susie: OK. (goes out)

(Afterwards, the teacher has the class rate how well they showed accepting in the role-play).

Teacher: OK, everyone rate Susie and Mark. Rate Susie with your left thumb and Mark with your right thumb. If you think they were accepting, give a thumbs up. If you think they were mostly accepting, but left something out, give a medium thumbs. If you think they didn't show accepting, give a thumbs down. (Students rate). Leslie, why did you give a thumbs up?

Leslie: Because I thought they went out right after they were called out and had calm bodies and calm voices.

Teacher: I thought so to. Mark frowned a little bit, but that's OK as long as he doesn't yell or refuse to go out. Susie and Mark, you both showed all the parts of accepting. Good job. Here are your points for participation. (Teacher now gives instructions to the class for the upcoming game.) The game you will be playing today is freeze tag. In this game, you will have lots of chances

to show accepting. Before we play, let's have everyone make predictions on the thermometer. How do you think you will do? Do you think you're going to break the thermometer today with all of your good social skills?

Students (in unison)**:** Yes!

Teacher: I hope you do too! I'll be looking for accepting today. I'm also looking for good sports. Let's play. (Game begins. Students show good accepting during the game.)

After the game is over:
Teacher: How do you think you did?

Students: We broke the thermometer!

Teacher: I saw a lot of accepting out there today. I agree! You broke the thermometer. That will be 100 extra good sport bucks for the group! How did you like playing the game today when everyone was accepting?

Students: It was fun!

Teacher: It's usually more fun when everyone is accepting. Now remember, I'm going to be watching for accepting all week.

Using Problem-Solving
Many ADHD children respond impulsively and don't think about the many options they have for handling difficult situations. They act before thinking. One approach for changing this is to teach the children how to solve problems—that is, teach them to think before acting. At the UCI-CDC school, students are taught specific steps to solve problems. The steps are:

> 1. What's the problem?
> 2. What are my choices?
> 3. Pick one.
> 4. Do it.
> 5. Did it work? If it did, pat yourself on the back. If not, go back to step 3.

Whenever a problem occurs, the student is taught to signal a "T" with his hands, which means he is calling a time-out for problem-solving. The teacher then guides the student through the problem-solving steps. The student is told to think of at least three choices. One choice may be a "high risk" choice, which means that it will probably lead to more problems. The others should be "low risk" choices, which have a greater chance of a positive outcome. The student selects one of the low risk choices to do, does it, then evaluates how it worked. Here is an example:

1. **What's the problem?** Sean hit me.
2. **What are my choices?** Hit him back (high risk choice), tell the teacher, walk away.
3. **Pick one.** *Not a high risk choice;* tell the teacher.
4. **Do it.** (Eric tells the teacher who then tells the two boys to discuss the problem. The teacher tells Sean to sit out one game for hitting.)
5. **Did it work?** If it did, pat yourself on the back. If not, go back to step 3.

This approach gives the students an opportunity to think carefully about what happened rather than simply react in the moment. Better solutions are the result. Take note: ADHD students often don't do problem-solving on their own, even after learning the steps. They need lots of supervision and reinforcement to use this approach consistently. For more information about problem solving interventions, refer to *Cognitive-Behaviorial Therapy with ADHD Children* (see References).

Chapter Three

Individualized Behavior Programs: When More Is Needed

Until now, we have discussed basic interventions useful for the entire classroom. These interventions are part of what's considered good classroom management. Most students respond to these basic strategies, but ADHD students often need more. This section is specifically designed for those cases needing more potent interventions. These interventions can be administered by a single teacher using the parallel teaching approach (teach, scan, intervene), but in some cases, a classroom aide trained in behavioral interventions allows a more intensive application of the intervention.

Assessing Behavior

The first thing you will need to do is specify very clearly what the problem is and what may be triggering and maintaining it. Why is this so important? The reason is based on the fact that ADHD students are quite diverse in terms of the problems they exhibit, the cause of their problems, and their response to different behavioral interventions. We need to know the specific problems a child exhibits before we can design effective behavior change programs.

Define the behavior of concern.

Problems may arise due to too much inappropriate behavior (e.g., interrupting) or too little appropriate behavior (e.g., not completing enough work). Be very specific and clear about the problem. Translate global personality traits into observable, specific behaviors. For example, "laziness" might be defined as "not completing assigned work;" bossiness might be defined as "name-calling" or "making demands of others," and forgetfulness might be defined as "failing to turn in completed homework." Why is it important to be so specific? Behaviors are easier to change than personality traits. Behaviors are easier for people to agree about. Behaviors are also more objective and less susceptible to bias.

Once you have identified the problem you are concerned about, you are ready to identify what may be triggering and maintaining it. Identify what happens right before the problem occurs. These are things that may have precipitated or set off the problem. Ask yourself whether the problem behavior generally occurs:

1. at the same time of day?

2. while a specific subject is being taught?

3. when a certain task is given?

4. when a particular instruction format is in effect: group lesson, individual seatwork, center-focused activities, cooperative learning activity, etc.?

5. when the student is around certain peers?

6. in response to a classmate's provocation?

7. in response to a direction from you?

8. at recess or other less structured times of the day?

9. when the student is overstimulated or excited?

10. when the student is bored?

Identify what happens right after the problem behavior occurs. These are things that can maintain the problem. When the problem behavior occurs or the desired behavior fails to occur, ask yourself whether the student:

1. gets out of doing any work?

2. gets attention from peers (be it positive or negative)?

3. gets his or her way?

4. gets someone to do an undesired/difficult task for him or her?

5. sees you get frustrated or angry? (This can be a reinforcer.)

6. disrupts the class?

7. gets positive attention from you? (For example, some teachers try to discourage off-task behavior with comments such as: "I know you can behave better. Is something wrong?" This kind of response can reinforce the problem.)

Monitoring behaviors and keeping records.

The best way to find out what sets off or maintains problems in a given situation is to keep a written record, like the one below, of what was going on just prior to and just following the problem behavior for several days.

Day	Problem behavior	What was happening when it occurred?	What happened just after it occurred?
Monday	Andy tipped his chair over and fell.	Students were taking turns at reading sections of their history books while the others followed along	The students near Andy laughed. I told Andy that it wouldn't have happened if he had been sitting properly. He seemed to enjoy the attention. I became angry.

After you have tracked the behavior for a few days, you can look for patterns (Does it always seem to happen at the same time? Is the child usually successful in getting the attention of his peers or a negative, emotional reaction from you?). Based on what seems to trigger or maintain the problem, you can decide on interventions. For example, if the problem behavior is always followed by the same thing (e.g., the student ends up getting out of doing some of his work), the most effective intervention may be to change the consequence to the behavior (e.g., make sure the student has to complete all assigned work before earning basic privileges such as recess). Likewise, if the problem is always set off by the same thing (e.g., a difficult task), the most effective intervention may be to modify that which sets it off (e.g., break the task down into smaller parts that are easier to understand). If the problem seems to occur because the student is trying to avoid doing certain tasks, you might try changing the task in a way to make it more enjoyable or have the student earn a privilege for completing the task. Sometimes it is hard to know exactly what is causing any given problem. If you don't see any particular patterns don't give up! There are many strategies that work even when you are not sure of the exact cause of the problem.

It is usually a good idea to find out how often or for how long the problem occurs before you start a behavior change program. This is called getting a baseline of the behavior. Getting a baseline may take some time, but it is important to be as objective as you can in observing the behavior. It is all too easy to overestimate the frequency of a problem when it is highly disruptive, or particularly annoying to us. We also tend to overestimate problems as a function of our own moods, levels of stress, and so on. Similarly, we can also underestimate the frequency of a problem. We may be especially vulnerable to this when the behavior is not very disruptive (e.g., daydreaming). Knowing how often or for how long the problem behavior occurs before you start an intervention will also help you set fair and realistic goals for the student.

To find out how often a behavior occurs you can simply keep a tally:

Behavior	9:00-10:30	10:30-12:00	12:00-2:00
Interruptions			
Raised hand			

To find out how long a behavior lasts, you can keep track of the duration of each occurrence:

	Length of successive occurrences of behavior				
Behavior	1	2	3	4	5
Out of seat	15 minutes	5 minutes			
Worked on assignment	10 minutes out of 30 minutes				

Selecting Target Behaviors and Goals

Once you have defined the problem, you are ready to select specific target behaviors. Target behaviors are those behaviors you would like the student to be doing instead of the problem behavior. For example, if the problem is being disruptive during independent seatwork, the target behavior might be completing work quietly. If the problem is fighting, the target behavior might be getting along with others.

Here are some popular target behaviors for ADHD students:

● Follows directions: follows directions given by teacher within reasonable period of time

● Follows class rules: e.g., sits properly and remains seated unless given permission to leave seat; talks only when given permission by teacher

- Completes class work: completes assigned work accurately and neatly

- Works quietly: no talking or noise making without teacher permission

- Keeps desk clean: desk area is organized and clean at specified check points

- Completes homework: completes and turns in homework with acceptable accuracy and neatness

- Gets along with peers: gets along with peers without teasing or fighting

- Gets started right away: starts work or assigned activity within time specified by teacher

Use these guidelines for selecting target behaviors and goals:

1. Start out simple. Have only one target behavior. However, if you use a token economy (described below) you may want to start with three or four target behaviors.

2. If the most important target behavior from your standpoint will be a difficult goal for the child, avoid the temptation to tackle that one first. It is important to start out successfully, so make sure these first behavioral goals are easy to achieve. You may start out implementing the program during the morning hours and then add the afternoon hours once the child shows improvement in the morning.

3. It is usually better to reward a positive behavior than to reward the absence of a negative behavior. Otherwise, you run the risk of not teaching the student a better alternative. For example, if the problem is calling out, it is better to reward handraising (the positive behavior), than the absence of calling out (the problem behavior). If you only reward not calling out, the student may inadvertently get reinforced for not participating at all. Notice how each of the target behaviors listed above is worded as a behavior to increase. (continued on the next page)

4. Whenever academic productivity is a problem, make sure to select an academic target behavior such as completing assignments or turning in complete homework. Don't just simply reward the student for staying on-task. If you do, work productivity may not increase. An additional benefit of rewarding academic performance is that it often improves behavior at the same time.

5. Involve students in setting their goals. Ms. Fran Martin finds it important to set goals with students, not for students. She explains that problems are like "roadblocks." She asks students what their roadblocks are (e.g., talking too much in class) and what ways they can think of to help themselves. She has kids complete their own goal sheets where they decide what they want to achieve. The more involved the students are in setting goals the more likely they are to achieve them.

6. Set the goal for the target behavior at a realistic level of performance—that is, a level at which you think the student can succeed. Gather baseline data to find out what the level is. That is, observe how often the student achieves the goal without your doing anything. For example, how long can the student work quietly? How many assignments does the student currently complete? How often is the student interrupting? How often is the student aggressive? Once you have an idea of this baseline of behavior, you can set a small, reasonable goal for the student. Some teachers plan to set the goal at no more than 20% better than the student is already doing. For example, if a student is not completing any work, set the goal at completing 20% of assigned work, rather than all of the work. If a student is interrupting 15 times a day, set the goal at no more than 10 interruptions. As the student shows improvement, the goal can and should be increased. But remember to focus on improvement not perfection!

Establishing Consequences

Once you've selected a target behavior and set the goals, the next step is to establish consequences for meeting or not meeting the goals.

In a previous section, we discussed the importance of positive attention and how to use your attention strategically to encourage appropriate behavior. Although positive attention can go far, it often does not go far enough for ADHD students. These students usually need more tangible, concrete rewards to inhibit their impulses and focus on the task at hand (Pfiffner & O'Leary, 1993). This usually means using activities, privileges, and/or token economies as rewards.

Using Activities and Privileges as Rewards

Activities and privileges that children enjoy are usually included as part of the normal routine in most classrooms. They can also be used as rewards to teach students good behavior and work habits. When used as rewards, certain activities and/or privileges are given only after a student meets a specific goal. For this to be effective, you must identify rewards that are meaningful to the student. There are several ways to do this:

- Consider what the student likes or asks to do.

- Observe what the child does when given free time. The things the child chooses to do are likely to be good rewards.

- Ask the student what he or she likes to do; ask what he or she would like to work for or earn. Use the survey on the next page.

- Take advantage of what's referred to as the Premack Principle. This principle states that a low probability activity (one that doesn't happen very often) can be increased by following it with a high probability activity (one that happens a lot). For example: One teacher found that completing assignments was a very low probability behavior for one ADHD student. On the other hand, a high probability behavior for this student was draw-

ing pictures. The student would spend all day drawing if it was left up to him. This teacher decided to use drawing time as a reward. For each assignment completed, the student earned a brief period of time drawing.

- If you can, use activities that double as good learning experiences. Mr. Agler calls these 2 for 1's. For example, he incorporates money lessons into a weekly movie theater reinforcer where kids watch a movie on a school TV. Kids use their points to buy movie tickets and snack bar items.

Here is a sample survey you can use to find out what activities and privileges a student likes.

Jennifer's Favorite Things at School

What classroom activities do you like best?

Art projects

What privileges do you like to have at school?

to be able to work in the office

What is the best prize your teacher could give you?

candy maker and stickers

What are your favorite food treats that you can have at school?

candy and nuts

What do you like to do most during free time at school?

talk to friends

Who do you like to spend your time with at school?

my friends

What would you like to do more often at school?

talk

Below is a list of activities, privileges, and tangible rewards that many teachers have found to be effective motivators for ADHD students.

Suggested School Rewards

Art/craft project (sidewalk art, mask-making, exhibitions)

Baseball cards

Being teacher's helper

Being the class monitor

Blow pops

Bringing in something from home

Certificates/awards

Choosing where to sit in class

Colorful pencils

Cooking

Eating lunch in special area

Erasing chalkboards

Extra "free" time

Extra computer time

Extra recess or extra lunch

Field trips

Free reading

Free time with friend

Fun erasers

Game of hangman

Games in class

Good note home to parents

Grab bag with small toys or school supplies

Gum

Having a classwork or homework pass

Helping correct papers

Librarian for the day

Lining up first

Listening to tape player/music

Lotteries/raffles

Lunch with a friend

Lunch with the teacher or principal

Making something for bulletin board

Movies in class

Picking another student with whom to do something

Removing the lowest grade or making up a missing grade

Running errands

Sitting in special area of class (bean bag chairs)

Snacks or other food treats

Stamps

Stickers

Stuffed animal to adopt for the night

Taking care of class animals

Treasure chest

Treasure hunt

Writing on chalkboard

Setting Up an Activity-Based Reward Program

Below is a worksheet to help you design an individual program using activities and privileges as rewards. Note that ADHD students need immediate rewards. Have students earn the activity or privilege on a daily basis for the most positive result. Here is a sample of a program developed by a teacher to address a student's disruptive behavior during math period.

---

1. What is the behavior I'm concerned about? Be specific.
noise making

2. How often does it happen? (the baseline)
several times each math period

3. What do I want the student to be doing instead? (the target behavior)
working and being quiet

4. How many times, or for how long must the student do the target behavior to earn a reward?
Kevin has to be quiet and do his work for most of the math period. He can have two reminders to be quiet and still earn the reward

5. What activity or privilege can be used as a reward? (Get input from the student.)
reduction in math homework

6. When will the reward be given? (Remember, immediate feedback is most effective.)
Kevin will get a homework pass right after math period is over

---

Using Token Economies

Token economies are another way to teach positive behaviors. In a token economy, students earn tokens such as points, stars, or tickets throughout the day and then later exchange their earnings for what are called "back-up" rewards. The "back-up" rewards are usually privileges, activities, or tangibles like those listed above. Tokens are especially effective for ADHD students because they can be given right away and often. The back-up rewards can be interesting and varied, and the token bridges the gap between the student's good behavior and the reward. Also, you can use tokens for several different target behaviors.

Follow these steps for setting up a token economy:

1. Identify one to four "target" behaviors you want to change.

2. Select the kind of token to use. Younger children often enjoy tangible tokens such as poker chips, stamps, or color cards. Older children do well with points.

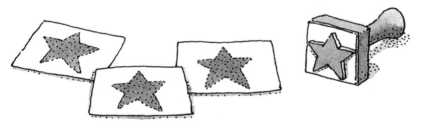

3. Establish times each day for giving the student feedback about the number of tokens earned. This is usually several times a day (e.g., before recess, before lunch, before dismissal). For high rates of problems or younger children you may want to provide feedback as often as every half hour.

4. Decide on "back-up" rewards that tokens can buy. Use a range of privileges and activities listed in the form of a "reward menu" to make sure there is enough variety and novelty. Remember that what is reinforcing to one

Rewards

Games in class	4 tokens
Gum	2 tokens
Extra free time	3 tokens
Being teacher's helper	3 tokens
Choosing where to sit	4 tokens

child may not be reinforcing to another. Also, only use rewards that can be withheld if not earned. For example, if activities such as art, sports, or free time cannot be withheld, don't use them as rewards.

5. Set the token value for each target behavior and the purchase price for rewards. Target behaviors can be weighted according to difficulty level. Target behaviors that are easy for the child to accomplish can be worth fewer points than more difficult ones. The purchase price for the rewards should be set at a level that doesn't exceed the child's spending power. Don't make it necessary for a child to earn all possible tokens to get a reward. Instead, have rewards available for improvement. The child should be able to be successful right away so that he or she feels confident and stays interested in the program.

6. Give both the opportunity to earn a daily reward based on that day's point total (e.g., extra computer time) and a longer-term reward such as a weekly reward based on the week's total (e.g., free time with a friend, grab bag). Weekly rewards are sometimes based on the number of good days during the week or the total number of tokens earned.

7. Use a chart to keep track of tokens earned each day. Here is an example:

Classroom Challenge

Student: _____ Day: _____

2=Very good
1=OK
0=Needs improvement

Times Assessed:	Behavior 1:	Behavior 2:	Behavior 3:
before RECESS	0 1 2	0 1 2	0 1 2
before LUNCH	0 1 2	0 1 2	0 1 2
before DISMISSAL	0 1 2	0 1 2	0 1 2

Total points earned:

Signatures: _____   _____
　　　　　　　　　　　Teacher　　　　　　　　　　　　Student

Rewards:

Comments:

As shown, charts should include the day of the week, space to list the target behaviors, and space to record the number of tokens (points, in this case) earned. On this chart there is also space to list rewards that points can buy. All parties involved can sign the chart to make it an official contract.

Let's look at how a teacher might set up a token economy and review it with a student:

Teacher: Michael, there are some areas at school in which I think you could do better, and I'd like to go over a program I think might help you. (Teacher pulls out above chart and reads the contents as the student looks on.) These are the areas that I think you could do better in: Following directions—which means doing what I ask right away; Completing assignments—which means doing all of the assigned work by the time you are supposed to; and Raising your hand—which means raising your hand instead of blurting out when you have something to say. Now, I've set it up so you can get up to two points for each of these three areas three times a day—before recess, before lunch, and before dismissal. We'll record your points on this card. So how many points can you earn each day?

Michael: I can earn six points three times a day, so that comes to 18 points that I can earn a day.

Teacher: That's right! What's your favorite privilege that you would like to work for if you get 17 or 18 points?

Michael: Free reading on the bean bag chair.

Teacher: OK, that sounds good. You can earn the free reading during our study hall period. How about if you earn 14, 15, or 16 points? That's still a pretty good day overall.

Michael: Computer lab.

Teacher: That's fine. If you get less than 14 points that means that you had a lot of problems that day. So you wouldn't earn any special privileges. You would just have regular study hall at your desk. To make sure I know you understand, tell me how this program works.

Michael: First I have to work on following directions, completing my work, and raising my hand. We'll check the chart before recess, before lunch, and before dismissal. If I get 17 or 18 points, I get free reading. If I get 14, 15, or 16 points, I get computer lab. Otherwise, I have regular study hall.

Teacher: I think you have it. How do you think you will do?

Michael: Good. I think I can get all 18 points.

Teacher: Great, let's start on Monday.

Michael starts the program the next school day. He brings the card to his teacher for signature at the end of the three rating periods. See the card on the following page.

Here is what the teacher says to him at the end of the last rating period.

Teacher: You earned two points for following directions, and two points for completing your work, but you forgot to raise your hand several times, so you won't get a point for raising your hand. Let's count up all of your points.

Michael: It comes to 16 points.

Teacher: That's right. What's the one area you need to improve tomorrow?

Michael: Raising my hand.

Teacher: That's right. You did well for the first day; keep up the good work! You can go to computer lab now.

Classroom Challenge

Student: _Michael_   Day: _Monday_

2=Very good
1=OK
0=Needs improvement

Times Assessed:	Behavior 1: Following directions	Behavior 2: Completing assignments	Behavior 3: Raising hand
before RECESS	0 1 ②	0 1 ②	0 1 ②
before LUNCH	0 1 ②	0 1 ②	0 1 ②
before DISMISSAL	0 1 ②	0 1 ②	⓪ 1 2

Total points earned: _16_

Signatures: _Mrs. Smith_   _Michael_
               Teacher   Student

Rewards:
17 or 18 points=free reading on bean bag chair
14-16 points=computer lab
Less than 14 points=study hall

Comments: _Great start!_

Keys to Success when Implementing a Token Program:

1. Be consistent. Don't forget about the program, adhere to the criteria set for tokens, and don't give in.

2. When tokens are earned, provide praise, be enthusiastic, and be sure to follow through. For example: "You did a great job following all the rules today!" Don't say to a student that a token or back-up reward was earned and then later refuse to give the reward because you are upset about some other unrelated problem that came up.

3. When tokens are not earned or are lost, don't lecture or argue with the student. Be matter-of-fact and brief. You may want to ask the student what he or she needs to work on to earn tokens the next day. Example: "You didn't get your math assignment done today so you don't earn any points. What do you think you can do tomorrow to do better?"

4. Use both daily and longer-term (e.g., weekly, biweekly) rewards. If rewards are only earned once per week (or less), many ADHD students will lose interest in the program.

Individual and Class-Wide Reward Programs

Reward programs can be set up for individual students, for groups of students, or for the entire class. Individual programs or class-wide programs wherein students earn rewards for their own behavior are usually best for the ADHD student. Many teachers prefer doing class-wide programs since they have found that rewards improve the performance of all children and are easier to use if used for all. Other teachers like to concentrate their efforts on individual children. In either case, designing these programs is part science and part art. Be creative and imaginative; the more enthusiastic you are, the more motivated the students will be.

Here are some examples of individual and class-wide activity/privilege programs:

Peg system: Ms. Cheryl Crosswait taught kindergarten-first grade ADHD students at the UCI-CDC school and used a "peg system" when an individual child was having problems.

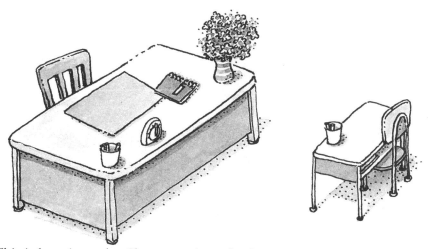

This is how it works: She sets a timer for between two and five minutes (the length depends on how frequently the problem occurs—for frequent problems, the time should be brief, for less frequent problems the time can be longer). If the child follows all classroom rules until the timer goes off, the child earns a peg kept in a cup. Whenever the child breaks a rule, the teacher gives herself a peg kept in a separate cup and then resets the timer. At the end of the period (often about an hour in length), pegs are counted. If the child has more pegs than the teacher, the child earns an activity or selects an activity for the class to do. If the teacher has more pegs, the teacher selects the activity for the class and the child does not participate. As the student is successful with just a few minutes, the time length is increased.

Stamps: Another strategy Ms. Crosswait likes to use is having students earn stamps when they are working. She uses stamps that are fun for kids like a picture of a bee which she gives to students who are working as "busy as a bee." She walks around the class during independent work time and stamps the work of students who are working hard. She uses a different

stamp for each period/subject which increases the value of each stamp. For an added twist, you can have each stamp be worth a ticket in a lottery at the end of the week.

Basketball shots: An easy activity to use for a reward is "shooting hoops" in class. One fourth grade teacher has a portable basketball hoop in her class. She has students earn shots for things like completed assignments, reciting a poem to the class, and participating in class discussions. Teachers at UCI-CDC improvise by using a nerf ball and buckets for hoops and have kids earn shots for positive social skills.

On-task thermometer: This is a variation of the Goodsport Thermometer discussed earlier. Here, a picture of a thermometer is placed on the student's desk. When the student is on-task, the temperature reading is raised. When the student is off-task, it's lowered. For periods of time in which the thermometer shows a high temperature, the student earns time doing a special activity of his choice at the end of the day (e.g., playing a game, drawing with special markers, helping the teacher). If the thermometer becomes so hot (the student is doing so well) that it "breaks," the time is doubled. For periods in which the thermometer is at the lowest point, the student earns detention time after school.

Privileges for completed work: Students who complete work with time to spare before the next activity can earn extra free time, free reading, or simple art projects. Mr. Agler has his kindergarten-first grade students earn time playing a computer game when they finish an assignment. He makes this attractive by having kids preview the "game of the day" ahead of time. Ms. Bain finds that modifying homework requirements can be a very effective reward for her second and third grade students. One way she does this is by having students earn the privilege of doing homework during the last 20 minutes of class instead of doing it at home. At other times she has students earn homework passes that they can turn in on one day of their choosing. On that day, students are excused from their homework assignment.

Here are examples of class-wide token economy programs:

Center rewards: Norrie Hirsch's second grade students at P.S. 182 in the Bronx, NY, earn points every day for behaviors such as completing assignments correctly, walking from the class to exit quietly, following class rules, appropriate lunchroom behavior, reading quietly during silent reading, etc. Ms. Hirsch writes down the points each child earns on 3" x 5" cards located in each child's journal. Twice per week children can exchange their points for time at a center of their choosing such as the housekeeping center (the most popular), the school center, or the transportation center. A maximum of four people is allowed at each center to make sure the activity stays under control and fun for all.

Tickets in a jar: Suzanne Vighetti uses "good behavior" tickets as an incentive for all her kindergarten students (usually over 20 students are in a class) at Franklin Elementary School in Bethel Park, PA. Children earn tickets for things like putting their name on their papers, sitting up straight and listening, and coloring neatly. They write their name on tickets they earn and put them in a class jar. Ms. Vighetti draws tickets from the jar at random times during the day. Children whose tickets are drawn earn rewards such as going

to the office, being first in line, getting the mail or a prize from the prize box (pencils, erasers, trinkets, seasonal things). She adds an element of surprise to the program by "sneaking up" behind students and giving them tickets privately while they are working. She also sometimes staples a ticket onto a student's good work. She varies how she uses the ticket system depending upon the needs of her class, but usually finds it important to have ticket drawings every day (and sometimes several times a day) especially at the beginning, to keep her young students motivated.

Ticket system with weekly and monthly rewards: Ms. Shirley LaCroix teaches second grade at Killybrooke Elementary School in Costa Mesa, CA. She uses tickets to reward the good behavior of all of her students. Each day she sets daily goals with her class. They usually focus on the rule that needs the most work. All students can earn tickets for following the rule of the day and for other things like doing their homework, doing their work neatly, working quietly, following directions right away, helping others, and lining up properly. She also has individual behavior goals for children who need them. These might be things like completing a spelling assignment, telling the truth, or fol-

lowing directions. She adjusts her expectations for ADHD students as necessary by rewarding students who are trying hard, even if they are not behaving perfectly. She gives out tickets frequently during the day and also likes to give impromptu tickets. Ms. LaCroix wears clothes with pockets so she can carry the tickets wherever she goes and can give a student a ticket at a moment's notice. Every Friday, students trade their tickets for treats. Once a month she brings down her special box which contains bigger treats like stickers, tattoos, crayons, pens, baseball cards, and other little trinkets that can be traded for tickets.

Kid-bucks with an auction: Mr. Teeman uses a kid-bucks system in his fifth grade class. All 33 students earn dollars every day for being responsible, being well behaved, showing good academic skills, working together, and for individual goals in areas of need. They also earn dollars for completing projects and getting good grades. Students can also get paid for doing a variety of "jobs" in class like being a teacher's helper, cleaning up the class library, being an office monitor, passing out items, and helping someone on the computer. Students can lose dollars for talking, not turning in homework, and not taking their turn to be a play leader. Students spend their dollars at class auctions. They can buy things like stickers, candy, baseball cards, posters, and comics.

Model token economy for ADHD students in a small class setting: A school-wide token program, designed specifically to meet the needs of ADHD students, is in effect at the UCI-CDC school program (Swanson, 1992). At this school (which exclusively serves ADHD students), the token economy serves as the backbone of the behavior management program (other interventions, including social skills training, are described in other sections of this book). The token economy is in place in the combined kindergarten-first grade, second-third grade, and fourth-fifth-sixth grade classrooms. Each class contains a maximum of 15 students taught by one teacher and one aide. The school day is divided into 30-minute periods. Students earn a maximum of 20 points each period for the following behaviors: getting started on their work, following directions, following class rules, staying on-task, getting along with peers, and cleaning up. During each period, students are told when they are earning or not earning points. At the end of each period is a "point check" where students are told how many points they have earned or what color patrol they have earned. Color patrols correspond to points earned as follows: Red patrol=90% or more of possible points earned; yellow patrol =80-89% of possible points earned; blue patrol=below 80% of possible points earned. Points and percentages are emphasized with the older students; color

patrols are emphasized with the younger students. Students' earnings are posted on a board displayed in class.

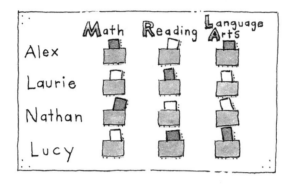

In the 2-3 and 4-5-6 grades, students also report how well they think they did. If their self-rating matches the teacher's rating, they earn bonus points. During the last 20 minutes of the day, students earn reinforcement, based on their earnings that day. The higher their earnings, the greater the number of choices they have for reinforcement. Students earning red patrol, or 90% or more of possible points, have the most choices. They can choose from all centers and reinforcement activities such as computer time, "red patrol" games, art supplies (the favorite ones), outside play, or any of the activities listed for the other levels of reward. Students earning yellow patrol or 80-89% of points possible earn fewer choices which include: watching (but not playing) any red patrol activity, "yellow patrol" games, art supplies (less favorite ones), card games, and puzzles. Students earning blue patrol, or less than 80% of points possible, have the fewest choices. They stay at their seats and read or write with pencils and paper.

Students also earn weekly rewards based on the week's total. Weekly rewards might be movies, taco fests, pizza, water play, special games, special art projects, or field trips. Students also progress through a levels system based on their ability to maintain positive behavior (i.e., red patrol

behavior) over an extended period of time. Increased privileges are provided for maintaining responsible and appropriate behavior and moving up the levels. All students start at Level 1 where they receive the fewest basic privileges and the most feedback. After one to two weeks of red patrol and correct matches (older students only), they move to Level 2 which includes increased privileges, such as lining up second, increased area to eat at lunch, and access to "Level 2 chairs" (ones in a more desirable location). After another couple of weeks of earning red patrol, they advance to Level 3. At Level 3 the frequency of feedback is reduced and students earn privileges such as lining up first, sitting in "Level 3 chairs" (ones in the most desirable locations), eating in area of choice, and being a teacher's helper. Students can also move through a challenge level and a transition level which serves as a way to gradually "fade out" the program. This is a very intensive program and is most needed when working with severe ADHD students. Having a small class size and having an aide assist each of the three teachers at the school helps make the program work. However, teachers of general education classes with up to 30 students (but only a few having ADHD), have implemented modifications of this program with success.

Using classroom aides to implement a token economy in the general education classroom: With ADHD students who require very frequent monitoring and feedback, a classroom aide may be necessary to assist the teacher in implementing the token economy. The Irvine Paraprofessional Program was developed by Dr. Ronald Kotkin at the UCI-CDC as a way to provide this kind of intensive intervention for severe ADHD students in the general education classroom (Kotkin, 1995). A major part of the program utilizes an adaptation of the school-wide token economy at the UCI-CDC (described above) in the context of strong support from administration. School psychologists consult with the teachers to initially develop the token economy (and assist teachers in using other general management strategies).

Paraprofessionals, with extensive training in behavioral interventions, serve as classroom aides to assist with the implementation of the token economy. The paraprofessionals implement the token economy with up to three identified students during morning hours. The teacher operates the token economy in the afternoon. The child receives tokens (stamps) for up to four target behaviors during designated time periods as indicated on the sample form below. When the paraprofessionals are in the class, the time period is every 15 minutes. In the afternoon when the teacher is implementing the program, the time periods are longer (45 minutes) to make the program more practical for the teacher to do. In addition to the feedback at the end of each period, students are given one to three reminders during each period to do the target behavior.

At the end of the day, students bring their daily report cards to a school-based reinforcement center where the stamps they have earned on the card are exchanged for a choice of a 20-minute activity. The more points earned, the greater the choice of activities (computer games are popular). A sample daily report card is on page 103.

The program also includes a three-tier levels system where students earn privileges as they move up each of three levels by consistently reaching daily and weekly goals. The levels system also provides a mechanism to fade the program since feedback intervals are increased (e.g., from 15 minutes to one hour) and the frequency of reminders are reduced as students achieve higher levels. The goal is to fade the program to a level in which the teacher can take over without assistance from the paraprofessional and still maintain the student's positive behavior. In addition to the token economy, students participate in social skills groups (similar to those described on page 67) led by the paraprofessionals twice a week. Rewards in the form of parties and games are provided for showing good social skills.

Jason's Classroom Challenge

Morning Schedule 8:00-12:00

On-Task Behavior

Staying Seated: Receive one stamp every 15 minutes that you remain seated. Getting out of seat with teacher's permission is OK.

8:15	8:30	8:45	9:00	9:15	9:30	Snack
10:15	10:30	10:45	11:00	11:30	11:45	

Working Quietly: Receive one stamp every 15 minutes if you do not visit with your neighbor or make distracting noises or gestures. Visiting neighbor with the teacher's permission is OK.

8:15	8:30	8:45	9:00	9:15	9:30	Snack
10:15	10:30	10:45	11:00	11:30	11:45	

Academic Performance

Amount of Work Completed: Receive one stamp every 15 minutes, if you complete assigned work during that period. During class discussions, stamps will be awarded if you are paying attention to the activity.

8:15	8:30	8:45	9:00	9:15	9:30	Snack
10:15	10:30	10:45	11:00	11:30	11:45	

Accuracy of Work: If 90% or more of work is completed accurately and your work is neat you will receive one stamp every 15 minutes. During class discussions, stamps will be awarded if contributions are accurate or task-related.

8:15	8:30	8:45	9:00	9:15	9:30	Snack
10:15	10:30	10:45	11:00	11:30	11:45	

Afternoon Schedule 12:45-2:00

Staying Seated: Earn 4 stamps every half hour that you remain seated.

1:15   1:45

Working Quietly: Receive 4 stamps every half hour if you do not visit with your neighbor or make distracting noises.

1:15   1:45

Amount of Work Completed: If you complete all work assigned you will receive 4 stamps every half hour.

1:15   1:45

Accuracy of Work: If 90% or more of work is completed accurately and is neat, you will receive 4 stamps every hour.

1:15   1:45

Total stamps possible= 80   Total stamps earned: _____

Reward

72 or more stamps = 90% Computer games
64 to 71 stamps = 80%   Free reading
66 to 70 stamps = 70%   Study hall

Group Rewards

So far we've talked mostly about rewards that children can earn for themselves. You can also set up group reward programs where each student works toward earning a reward that the whole class shares. More and more teachers are using these kinds of programs; they can be both practical for teachers and fun for kids. When working toward a group reward, kids often encourage each other to be well behaved and are more inclined to ignore their classmates' negative behavior. After all, the better their classmates do, the sooner they earn the reward. If you do use group reward programs though, expect that ADHD students may also need rewards that are directly tied to their own behavior and not dependent on the class. Also be careful. Some kids may try to sabotage the program. Make sure that no single child can have this kind of control over the whole class.

When you first use a group reward, set it up so that students can earn the reward fairly quickly (e.g., within a week). When they see how fun and rewarding it is, you can increase the time and requirements for earning the next group reward. Never have group rewards take longer than a month to earn or students may lose interest. You should also have a way of depicting students' progress toward earning the reward. Some teachers use marbles in a jar; others post pictures and diagrams related to the reward on the wall.

Here are several examples of group rewards:

Table points: In Ms. LaCroix' class, students sit at individual desks that are pushed together into groups of five or six. Each group has a name picked by the students. Students can earn table points for getting along, keeping their area clean, and sitting quietly. When a table earns a certain number of points, the whole table earns a 10-minute "party" where kids can sit outside and eat peanuts, popcorn, or candy. It usually takes about two weeks to earn enough points for a party. You might also try using more immediate, low-cost rewards such as: the table who cleans up first gets to line up first for recess.

Row points: In Ms. Hall's third grade class, 32 students are seated in rows and can earn row points for staying on-task, putting work away promptly, following directions, and working quietly. Row points are tallied periodically on the front chalkboard. The rows with the most points earn things like no-homework passes, extra recess and free time, taking a friend to lunch, and computer time. After a few days of the program, Ms. Hall finds that simply lifting up a piece of the chalk for tallying points works like "magic" to prompt good behavior. She makes a point of changing everyone's seat every six weeks so that students are eventually grouped with everyone in the class. Ms. Hall also appoints a special person for the class every week. The "special person" gets to assign row points, excuse students to recess, be the hall monitor, run errands, and do special jobs in class. This would probably work well as a reward in and of itself.

Gumballs for lining up. Mr. Agler has clear rules for a good line-up which include keeping hands and feet to self. For each line-up where the students follow all of the rules, they earn a gumball sticker on a picture of a gumball jar posted on the wall chart in class. When all empty gumballs have stickers, the class earns the privilege of chewing gum for 30 minutes during reading time.

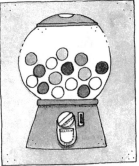

Parties: Theme parties are usually popular rewards. Parties can be brief (20-30 minutes) and are best done either at the end of the day or right before recess or lunch. One example described earlier is the pizza party, earned by students at the UCI-CDC school for showing good social skills. As another example, Ms. Bain has her students work for a nacho party. They earn paper tortilla chips for getting work done and staying on task. Students paste the chips they earn on a picture of a plate posted on a wall in class (see picture). Once the plate is full, the class earns a nacho party. Simple popcorn parties are also popular. You might try having kids earn

kernels of corn for good behavior. When the jar is full, pop the kernels earned at a popcorn party. As an alternative you can have kids pop their individual earnings to eat. *Suggestion:* Have the students' parents send in the food (or ingredients) for the parties.

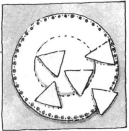

Treasure chest. Many teachers use trinkets from a treasure chest as rewards. Ms. Bain has a treasure chest in her class full of carnival prizes (bought in bulk) that she uses as a group reward. As a part of the

reward system, she has a picture of a ship sailing toward a treasure chest on an island posted in her room. For every 15 minutes that the class is working during independent seatwork (that's the most challenging time of the day), she moves the ship one inch closer to the treasure chest on the island. When the ship reaches the treasure chest, the class earns the reward (a trinket from the treasure chest for every student).

Movies: This popular activity can also be made into a group reward. Ms. Bain accomplished this in a creative and interesting way by hanging a

poster with a picture of students walking to a theater. The class progressed one inch closer to the theater for every 15 minutes they were working and on-task. When the students reached the theater, they earned the movie.

Teams and tournaments: Divide students into teams and have teams compete with each other to see who can earn the most points (tokens) in a day. You can increase the incentive value of the tokens by keeping daily tallies of points as though they were standings in a sporting league. If all teams achieve a certain goal, all should earn the reward.

Kathleen Healy, a fifth-grade teacher at M.S. 180 in the Bronx, NY, teaches in a departmentalized school, where there are six fifth grade classes of approximately 35 students each. Each class of students has five main teachers and classrooms to go to. In order to help all students be successful with multiple teachers and classrooms, a school-wide group reward is in place. The six classes compete against each other for class rewards. Rewards are earned based on points accumulated by each class. Teachers assign a grade (which are translated to points) to each class at the end of every period based on their overall behavior and work habits during that period. A "grade leader" for the fifth grade monitors the children closely and also distributes points during lunch, recess, and at other times when students may need help in remembering to follow the rules (e.g., when a substitute teacher is present). The grade leader keeps track of all of the points earned by each of the six classes. At regular intervals, the classes with the most points earn rewards such as special Friday recess, special trips, parties (pizza and soda parties are awarded four times a year to the class with the most points), treats (candy treats are awarded to classes with the second and third highest number of points at the quarterly reward period), and choice of where to sit during school movies. To maximize motivation, even for the more problematic classes, all classes earn a "first place" standing at some time during the year. To make sure this happens, the grade leader may set up special challenges such as the opportunity to earn bonus points during lunch or recess. Children with a pattern of behavior problems are prevented from sabotaging their class's success, since their point losses are not counted against the class. Instead, an individual daily school-home contract is set up for them. This school also has a student of the month program which gives an award to

one student per grade each month for "doing the right thing." This award is open to most students since students do not have to be excelling in the academic arena to earn the award.

Dealing with the Need for Novelty

ADHD students are notorious for losing interest in rewards. Expect and accept this. Probably the best way to deal with this need is to change rewards regularly. Plan on having to change some rewards at least every week or two. Using a reward menu (containing a list of potential rewards) and having students pick their own rewards can help increase variety. Changing the "packaging" of a reward is also recommended. This is something like good salesmanship and involves making the reward seem more fun and interesting by virtue of how you present it to the student. Many teachers know that novelty and presentation are often more important than cost. In many of the examples given above, the packaging was intentionally made to be captivating (e.g., using colorful posters depicting the reward the class was to earn: filling a gumball machine, walking to a theater, sailing to a treasure island). You might also consider using different reward themes corresponding to the time of year or an upcoming holiday. Themes can then be changed every month or so.

The words you use can also invite student interest. Call individual reward programs "special challenges" or "bonus rewards." Counselors at UCI-CDC have named special chairs that kids earn to sit in ("King's Chair"). They also call tokens (round colored stickers) earned for positive social skills "Big Deals" (they're a big deal to earn). Big deal earnings are posted on a wall chart and when the class earns a predetermined number, they have a fiesta. As a variation on this theme, Mr. Agler uses tokens he calls "Mystery Big Deals." The mystery is that he uses invisible ink to mark the number of points earned on a card (token). The child who earns the Mystery Big Deal scratches out the card to see how many points are earned. You could also write actual activities on the card for the child to scratch out. The child

would earn the activity written on the card. Another effective reward that was once used at the UCI-CDC involves having students earn clean-up duty. Clean-up duty was made to be a desired privilege by having students don white hats and coats, and call themselves the "clean-up crew." The students loved it! (These same kids probably hate cleaning their rooms at home.)

Using a Contract

You can formalize most any behavior program by writing up a behavior contract between you and the student. Contracts are particularly useful for older students. On the contract you should make it clear what your responsibilities are and what the student's responsibilities are. Also, if parents are involved in any way, their responsibilities should be included. You will probably find that students take the program more seriously if it is written in the form of a contract, especially if it involves their agreeing to the terms of the contract by signing it. Contracts can be made visually appealing, and help make the program seem more fun. Here is an example of a contract used by a fifth grade teacher:

Ben's Contract

I agree to work toward these goals:
complete my math assignment during math period
do the work neatly
turn in the assignment at the end of the period

If I meet my goals, I will earn: 15 minutes on the computer
If I do not meet my goals, I will not earn: computer time

_____   Date
Student's signature

I agree to monitor Ben's goals and give him the reward, if earned.

_____   Date
Teacher's signature

This part of the contract is included if parents are involved:

I agree to check Ben's report card daily and provide rewards at home if earned.

_____

Parent's signature   Date

Self-Monitoring and Self-Evaluation

Most of the programs discussed thus far have involved the teacher monitoring and evaluating students' behavior. However, the student can also be taught to monitor his or her own behavior. This skill is very important for ADHD youngsters since they are often impulsive and unaware of their own behavior and its impact on others. Researchers studying self-monitoring have found that having children earn rewards for accurate self-evaluations and positive behavior can be more effective than just having the teacher reward the positive behavior. Increasing the students' awareness of their own behavior can be done informally (e.g., "How do you think you did today?") or as part of a formal program (Shapiro & Cole, 1994). One formal program used with ADHD students is called "Match Game" (Hinshaw, Henker, & Whalen, 1984). This procedure involves having students rate their own behavior using descriptions, points, or colors over designated time periods. Younger children can rate more accurately when the rating categories are broad, so matching colors (not points) is recommended for them. Points should be reserved for older children (fourth grade and up). Extra points or a bonus are earned for ratings that match the teacher's ratings.

In the sample below, only one target behavior is used (although you can have several target behaviors). The student first provides his or her rating in the upper left corner of the box. Afterwards, the teacher gives his or her rating in the lower right corner of the box. If they match, bonus points are earned. If they do not match, the teacher rating is the one counted toward the reward.

Name: _____ **Day:** _____

I followed the class rules today

8:30-10	10-11:30	11:30-1	1-2:30

0=Not so good, didn't follow the rules
1=OK, followed most of the rules
2=Great, followed all of the rules

Matches:
Total points earned: _____
Teacher signature: _____

Some teachers have students rate themselves more often as a prompt to stay on-task and working. They might set a timer at random intervals and have the student check a box when the timer goes off if they have been working during that time or put a 0 if they had not. Teachers can give their rating below the student's rating.

I was doing my work:							
Student							
Teacher							

Once children learn the system, they are awarded points only when their behavior is good and their rating matches the teacher's rating. With practice, students as young as 7 or 8 can learn to rate their own behavior accurately. When student ratings are consistently accurate, teacher ratings can be gradually faded and, for some students, rewards can be based on the student self-ratings. However, teachers will still need to monitor the student ratings periodically (e.g., via random matching checks). Without monitoring, students can become overly lenient with their self-evaluations! You might also try having students predict how they think they will do before the activity and then see if their actual behavior matches their prediction (see sample on the next page). Having students make predictions can encourage positive behavior during the day (especially since most kids predict very successful days)!

Classroom Challenge with Student Predictions

Name: _____ Date: _____

Each category rated as follows: 2=Great!!
1=Fair; needed 1 or 2 reminders
0=Unsatisfactory

Target Behavior: attends to class discussions

9:00-11:00	11:00-12:30	12:30-2:30
Student prediction Teacher evaluation	Student prediction Teacher evaluation	Student prediction Teacher evaluation

Target Behavior: gets along with peers

9:00-11:00	11:00-12:30	12:30-2:30
Student prediction Teacher evaluation	Student prediction Teacher evaluation	Student prediction Teacher evaluation

Target Behavior: completes assigned work

9:00-11:00	11:00-12:30	12:30-2:3
Student prediction Teacher evaluation	Student prediction Teacher evaluation	Student prediction Teacher evaluation

Total points for a Great day: 15-18
Total points for a Fair day: 12-14
Total points for an Unsatisfactory day: 11 or less   _____
Bonus for matching: 2   Teacher's signature:
Total points earned: _____

Fading Reward Programs

To maintain the gains made from your reward program remove the program gradually and only after the behavior goals have been stable for at least several weeks or more. To fade a program:

- If you are using a token economy, reduce the frequency of token checks (e.g., from three times per day to once per day). This number can be further reduced (e.g., to once per week) as the student is successful.

- Modify the frequency and type of back-up rewards. For example, rewards can be given at the end of the week or every two weeks, instead of every day.

- Use fewer tangible rewards such as stickers or toys and use more activities and privileges instead.

- Have students earn their way off the reward program. Tell them that if they meet their goals for a certain period of time (at least several weeks), the program will be stopped. For older children, you may also require that the student continue to show accurate self-monitoring as the program is being faded.

Note: If behavior worsens when the program is being faded, the original system may need to be reintroduced. Also, keep in mind that for some ADHD students, a token system may need to be in place for months and even years to maximize academic and behavioral success.

The Prudent Use of Negative Consequences

Positive consequences, no matter how extravagant, usually do not get rid of the need for negative consequences. This may be especially true for impulsive and aggressive behavior and for very persistent or serious problems. The use of verbal corrective feedback (reprimands) was discussed in an earlier section. However, ADHD students often don't seem to be as responsive to such feedback as other students. They often need back-up negative consequences in

addition to the reprimand. This section describes the prudent use of three negative consequences—response cost, work tasks, and time-out.

Using Response Cost

Response cost refers to the process of taking away privileges, tokens, or activities as a consequence for misbehavior. When certain guidelines are followed, this has proved to be one of the most effective negative consequences for ADHD children.

There are many ways to set up response cost systems. For example, you might set up a system whereby students lose minutes off of a scheduled 20-minute free activity period at the end of each day for each aggressive act. Students who have no aggressive behavior earn the entire 20 minutes. Each aggression may result in a loss of five minutes of free time so that a student who is aggressive two times, loses ten minutes of free time. One teacher set up a response program using a music box to keep track of when students were following the rules. Whenever rules were not being followed the music was played. The number of minutes of music left at the end of the week corresponded to the number of minutes of free time earned by the whole class.

Another response cost approach involves giving students tokens at the beginning of the day. Tokens are then lost for certain misbehaviors. At the end of the day, children are "costed" based on the number of tokens they have lost. For example, a student might lose one minute of recess for every token lost. Another way to do this would be to have the student earn privileges based on the number of tokens kept. One teacher of a third grade class gave one of her students five points to start the day (see report on the next page). Every time the child called out she lost a point. For each point the child still had at the end of the morning, she earned two minutes on the computer.

Another system developed by Rapport, Murphy, and Bailey in 1982 involves using "flip cards." Flip cards are made from 20 hole-punched index cards that are attached by a ring. They are numbered from 1 to 20. One set

Behavior Report

Name: _____ Day: _____

Kept hands and feet to self: 1 2 3 4 5

Total points kept: ____ X 2 = ____ minutes computer time

Teacher's signature: _____

is kept at the child's desk and another at the teacher's. At the beginning of the day the child starts off with 20 on top. This represents 20 minutes of some privileged activity, such as recess. Each time the child breaks a rule, a card is flipped back so they have a visual reminder of how much time they have left for recess.

Some teachers use a color-card system whereby each student starts the day with a certain color card (often the color cards are kept in pockets on a chart in class). When the student breaks a rule or gets a warning for behavior, the color card is changed for that student and a consequence may be given. With each successive infraction, the color card is changed (usually up to three or four colors are used) and another consequence may be given. Some ADHD students may not improve their behavior with these programs. They may end up having problems early in the day, rapidly get color changes, and have nothing left to work for. For this reason, it is recommended that you have several opportunities for "fresh starts" during the day, especially for more problematic students. This is easily done by having colors start over each period (or several times a day). Students won't be able to change the color earned during preceding periods, but they can still work for a "better" color in later periods. The program description that follows is an example of an effective color-card response cost system.

Using response cost with ADHD kindergarten students: Dr. Russell Barkley at the University of Massachusetts Medical Center, along with Dr. Terri Shelton and Cheryl Crosswait, as part of a federally-funded project for ADHD kindergarten students, developed a comprehensive classroom management program using many of the strategies discussed in this book. One of these is a color-coded response cost program based on the UCI-CDC token economy described earlier (Shelton and Crosswait, 1992). In their program, one teacher and one aide taught up to 16 students per class. The students' behavior was reviewed every 30 minutes and students received a color card (red, yellow, blue) corresponding to how well they did. Students started "fresh" every 30 minutes with a red card (the best color). If they had an infraction, the color changed to yellow. If they had a severe infraction or several less severe infractions, the color changed to blue. Color strips were attached with Velcro to a board containing the students' names down one side and the periods listed across the top. Color earnings were totaled twice a day—once at the end of the morning and once at the end of the day—and exchanged for activity rewards. Those with mostly reds earned the most preferred activities, those with several yellows earned less preferred activities, and those with a blue earned the least preferred activities.

Having two reinforcement periods is helpful for this age. Weekly rewards, based on daily color earnings, were also provided. The program was faded successfully over the course of the year by gradually reducing feedback periods from twice per day to once a week, removing the chart from the class, and eliminating weekly rewards. Ms. Crosswait notes that the teachers found the system practical to use and were very positive about it (especially after seeing it work so effectively). She also reports that teachers of much larger kindergarten and first-grade classes (with up to 30 students) have also been able to implement the program easily, even without an aide in the class.

Many teachers like to use response cost with a reward-based token economy. In this arrangement, a student can both earn tokens and lose tokens.

For example, each of the teachers who use group reward programs described above also use response cost. In Mr. Teeman's class, students lose kidbucks for talking out of turn. In Ms. LaCroix' class, students lose tickets and table points when they break the rules. At the UCI-CDC school, points are lost for a number of behaviors such as not following directions and aggressive or destructive acts.

Response cost vs. reward: Many teachers wonder whether it is best to use response cost or a reward program. In other words, is it best to have students start with all their points (or reward) and then lose parts of it when problems occur, or is it better to have students start with nothing and have them earn it? Research studies show that both procedures can be effective (Pfiffner & O'Leary 1993). Response cost may be especially effective for aggressive and impulsive behavior since the student receives very immediate feedback directly related to the problem. For other behaviors, reward programs may be indicated. As an example, when trying to increase work productivity, it may be better to have students earn activities and privileges for completing their work, rather than losing privileges for not completing work. In this arrangement, a student who fails to complete work ends up not earning the privilege rather than losing the privilege. Framing programs in the positive way may decrease oppositional reactions. Consider the teacher's response in each of these approaches:

"You didn't complete your work so you don't earn free time today" vs. "You didn't complete your work, so you lost your free time today."

The latter wording may be more likely to entice arguments in some children. The decision about whether to use response cost or rewards also depends on the student. Some students are easily demoralized by losing points; others like the idea of starting out with all their points at the beginning of the day, rather than starting without any points. In many cases the combination of rewards and response costs is the most powerful approach.

Tips for using response cost:

1. Don't use this procedure arbitrarily. Plan in advance what behaviors will result in a loss and apply the consequence consistently. Make sure the student understands what behaviors will result in a "cost."

2. Use one warning before taking away the privilege. This helps the student learn the system and is generally associated with less defiance or complaints of unfairness. An if...then statement works well. For example: "If you don't start your work, then you will lose some time off of your recess."

3. When students are very angry, use an empathy statement to defuse the anger. "I know it is hard to stop in the middle of your game, but it is time to clean up."

4. Don't give more than one warning.

5. Incremental, rather than all-or-none losses work well. For example rather than losing all of recess, have the student lose a certain number of minutes of recess based on the severity of the infraction.

6. Make sure the privileges or activities lost are meaningful to the student. For example, although most students would mind losing recess, some students would prefer to stay inside. For those students, select another activity.

7. Stay calm. Don't use inflammatory language. Don't argue or lecture. Don't get too emotional, or spend too much time trying to explain yourself.

8. When possible, try to ignore whining and oppositional verbal statements. Provide consequences only for actual noncompliance. Sometimes expecting a student to change both behaviors at once is too much.

9. Not giving enough tokens to start with is one of the most common mistakes that teachers make with response cost. Also, set fair, realistic goals. After the student has been successful, the goals can be increased. An occasional day of losing all tokens may be effective, but if it is a pattern, the goal is too high.

10. Be sure to notice and comment on positive behavior. Using response cost sometimes results in more attention to negative behavior. Don't let this happen.

Using Work Tasks

Another procedure for handling misbehavior such as defiance, aggression, or damaging property, is assigning the student work tasks. This can prevent escalation of negative behavior and is a tool for helping the child regain self-control. One effective work task in use at the UCI-CDC school program involves administering simple, boring, purposeless marking tasks upon the occurrence of problem behavior. This task involves the student drawing a diagonal line through a series of ten small boxes on a sheet of paper.

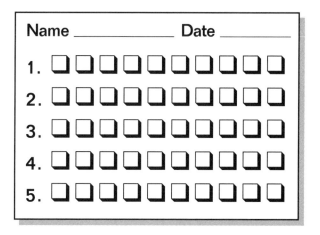

Another version of the task involves the student copying a series of numbers. Students can earn tasks for misbehavior, or they might earn tasks for not going to time-out promptly. Students may earn five tasks for certain infractions, 10 or even 20 tasks for more severe infractions. The teacher might say: "You're not following directions to go to time-out; that will be five tasks." If misbehavior continues, tasks are added by simply saying: "You are earning more tasks." When the child is sitting properly (at his or her seat or a special chair in the room used for doing tasks), he or she is given the task sheets to complete (they can be given one at a time). When the task sheets are complete, the teacher checks them for accuracy (lines must be diagonal) and then

discards them. Although this is a writing task of sorts, it has not been found to negatively influence a child's interest in academic work.

Using Time-Out

Time-out means time away from positive reinforcement. Time-out involves removing the student from opportunities to earn positive reinforcement like fun activities, peer attention, and teacher attention for a brief period of time. There are many ways to use time-out, such as removing work or materials from the student, or removing the student from preferred areas in the classroom to a time-out area. Another variation involves removing the opportunity to earn tokens for a period of time. One example of the latter is the Good Behavior Clock (Kubany, Weiss, & Sloggett, 1971). A clock runs whenever a student is on-task, but is stopped for a short period of time when a student is off-task or disruptive. While the clock is running, students can earn tokens or other rewards, but are not eligible for earning when the clock is stopped.

Steps for setting up time-out:

1. Select a time-out procedure. The options include: removing work materials, removing the opportunity to earn tokens or other rewards, or removing the student to an area in class that is free from reinforcing activities. A cubicle in the corner of the class works well.

2. Select a length of time. Usually two to three minutes is good to start. Extra time up to ten minutes may be added for students who refuse to go to time-out right away. An alternative is to start with ten minutes and then reduce the time if the student goes right away.

3. Select "back-up" consequences for failure to take a time-out or failure to follow time-out rules. Giving work tasks or taking away a privilege can be effective. For every minute a child refuses to go to time-out, he or she may have one minute after school or one minute off recess or one task.

4. Decide what behaviors will result in time-out. Common behaviors for time-out include: Aggression, repeated noncompliance, destruction of property, or general out-of-control behavior.

5. Describe the process to the student. "You have been doing a lot of hitting. We're going to start using time-out for hitting. That means whenever you hit or pretend to hit someone, you will have to go to the time-out chair at the back of the class."

6. Implement the procedure consistently, immediately, and calmly. Limit your talking to the student while he or she is in time-out. If the student is following time-out rules, don't say anything to the student. If the student is noncompliant and disruptive during time-out, calmly and briefly tell the student that he or she is earning work tasks or extra time, or losing privileges (e.g., for every minute of noncompliance during time-out, student loses one minute off recess or earns one minute after school detention). Do not argue with the student.

7. Classmates should be encouraged to ignore students in time-out. Those who choose to interact with the student should get a negative consequence.

8. When time-out is over, don't discuss it with the student. Simply give the student a direction as to what to do and reinforce the next appropriate behavior. Too much talking after time-out could end up reinforcing the problem.

What Makes Punishment Work?

Punishment works when it is brief, immediate, calm, and meaningful, and when lots of praise and rewards are given for positive behaviors.

Chapter Four

Parent and Teacher Partnerships

Working Together

Promoting a teacher-parent team spirit of cooperation is one of the best things you can do for an ADHD student. You will find that you will need to be more involved with parents of ADHD students, at least at the beginning of the year. Let parents know when problems first arise.

Parents can be a wonderful resource. Many are eager to become involved and support your efforts at school. Unfortunately not all parents provide the time and effort needed to effectively work with ADHD students. Some are ill-equipped to handle their child's behavior and are overly punitive. Others are multiply-stressed by life situations such as divorce, financial difficulties, unemployment, lengthy work hours, and family conflict. Compounding these problems, many parents with ADHD youngsters also have ADHD themselves. It is important to recognize that most parents of ADHD children have experienced the same kinds of difficulties with their child as you have. They are often equally frustrated and overwhelmed. In all likelihood, they have been made aware of their child's misbehavior and failure on many occasions over the years. Previous teachers have probably complained about the student, as have relatives, friends, and even strangers in supermarkets

and at parks. They may feel blamed for their child's problems and they may react defensively. They may seem to blame you for their child's problems. You may find yourself wondering if poor parenting is the root of the problem. Remember: ADHD is not caused by poor parenting, nor is it caused by particular teaching techniques. Don't give up too early with an uncooperative parent. Try to be patient, non-defensive, and encouraging when meeting with parents. Many will "come around" when other crises in their lives resolve or when they see your consistent efforts with their student.

What's the best way to communicate with parents and enlist their support in the educational process? Foster a team spirit. Show your commitment to working with the student. Stay problem-focused. Don't blame. Point out students' strengths. Communicate hope.

Keep parents informed about your class procedures. Give parents a list of classroom rules and procedures at the beginning of the year. Have them sign and return the list to you. Throughout the school year, keep parents abreast of any changes. You can also let them know how they can be helpful at home with their child's education. Tips about good books to read, educational programs to watch, places to go, and how they can best be involved with homework are all helpful. Refer to page 46 for more information about handling homework issues.

The Daily School-Home Report Card

The daily school-home report card is an excellent intervention for many ADHD students. It involves parents giving consequences at home based on the teacher's report of the child's performance at school. Teacher reports can be notes or more formal report cards with a list of the target behaviors and a rating for each behavior. The report card is usually sent home on a daily basis at first. Sometimes report cards are sent only on "good" days (i.e., when behavior or academic goals are met); in other cases report cards are sent on both "good" and "bad" days. After a period of success, the report cards can sometimes be faded to weekly, biweekly, monthly, and finally to the reporting

intervals typically used in school. However, in many cases, ADHD students benefit from having a daily or weekly report card in place for the entire school year. For more details regarding teacher-parent communication see Dr. Mary Lou Kelley's book entitled, *School-Home Notes.*

Advantages of using a school-home report card:

- Facilitates home-school communication
- Gives students more frequent feedback than usually occurs in class
- Prompts parents to reinforce good behavior
- The type and quality of reinforcers is greater at home than at school
- Requires less time for teacher than many in-class interventions
- Can be used as a record of student's progress
- Facilitates early detection of the need for problem-solving

Cautions in using a school-home report card:

Do not use a school-home report card if you are concerned about follow-through at home. Some parents do not have the skills necessary to reinforce consistently at home. In some cases, you may be concerned about overly punitive consequences. In these cases, consult with your school psychologist to try and locate a therapist who can provide assistance in child management skills for the family.

Also, don't use a school-home report card if the major problem is a learning disability or academic deficit. Sometimes adding incentives can increase frustration in a child who simply does not understand the academic material. School-home report cards are most effective when problems are due to motivational or attention deficits.

Note that these programs require that the student be able to delay gratification until they get home that day. For some students, this is not realistic. If behavior problems are severe, or the student needs more immediate rewards, you will need to supplement the school-home report card with rewards in class.

Steps for designing a reporting system:

The initial steps for setting up a school-home report card are much like those for setting up a token economy (since a school-home report card is essentially a token economy). Before meeting with the student and parents, identify a few target behavior goals you would like the child to achieve, collect a baseline rate of the behaviors, and set reasonable goals for the student. Then, design a "rough draft" of a reporting system to use. Several variations of school-home report cards are given.

Sample 1:

Includes two target behaviors rated three times a day and a rating of work completion. Space is provided for writing down the homework assignment and home rewards, and for the parent's signature.

_____ 's Day   Date _____

	8:30-10:00	10:00-11:30	11:30-1:00
Stayed seated with no more than 3 reminders			
Interrupted no more than 3 times			

Legend: 1= yes   0 = no

% of work completed correctly
(90-100%=4 points, 80-89%=3 points, 70-79%=2 points, less than 70%=0 points)

Homework for tonight:

Teacher's signature _____

Home Rewards:
9-10 points= basic and bonus privileges at home
7-8 points= basic privileges at home
less than 7 points=only inside activities at home (no basic or bonus privileges)

Parent's signature _____

Sample 2: Includes three target behaviors rated each period (or once at the end of the day), and space for listing test grades and homework.

Name _____ **Date** _____

Period/Time/Class _____

Followed class rules	all	some	none
Completed work	all	some	none
Turned in homework	all	some	none

Test grades
Homework

Teacher's signature _____

Sample 3: Includes two target behaviors for earning points, and one target behavior that results in a loss of points—numbers are crossed out for each instance of fighting (token economy with response cost)

Name _____

Period/Time/Class

Followed class rules	all	some	none
Completed work	all	some	none
Turned in homework	all	some	none

Test grades
Homework

Teacher's signature _____ Date _____

Meeting with the parent and the student:

1. Bring your list of target behaviors, your baseline records and sample report card to the meeting. Meet with just the parent first.

2. Open the meeting by setting the stage for cooperation. Point out the student's strengths and positive attributes.

3. Pinpoint specific problems in a non-blaming, non-ridiculing fashion.

4. Provide a rationale and describe the daily report card. Show samples of how one might look. The following is a script of how a teacher might present the report card system to a parent:

Teacher: Thank you for meeting with me today. I think it's best to meet early in the year so that we can make the year for Raul be the most successful it can be. First of all I want to say that I have really enjoyed Raul's enthusiasm and participation in class discussions. He seems to be very bright and very energetic. But I am concerned about some problem behaviors. Raul seems to be having trouble completing his work, and also spends too much time socializing with other students in the class. I have tried moving his seat so as to be away from his friends, but it doesn't seem to have solved the problem. I've also tried to make sure he understands the assignments. That doesn't seem to be a problem. At this point it seems that he just is not motivated to complete the work. One thing that I have found works well in these cases is a daily school-home report card or school-home note. In this system, we set up a few goals for Raul each day, like com-

pleting his assignments and following the no talking class rule. I keep track of his behavior in these two areas and send a note home to you to let you know how he did. If he did well, you would provide some reward for him at home. The reward might be something like special time with you, extra play time with friends, extra TV time. If he didn't do well, he wouldn't get the reward. Here is an example of how the report card might look (show copy) and here is a list of some rewards you might consider using. I have found this procedure to be very effective for many kids. What do you think about it? Does it seem like something you might be able to do?

5. Advise the parent to use basic privileges, not expensive, elaborate rewards. Emphasize the advantages of using privileges and activities as rewards instead of always relying on tangible rewards (low cost, always on hand, renewable). Also, tell parents to avoid using rewards they cannot withhold if not earned. For example, if the whole family is going to the ball game over the weekend regardless of the child's behavior, they should not use the ball game as a reward. The negative consequence for poor ratings is usually not earning the reward. However, additional negative consequences (e.g., early bedtime, loss of playtime) can be applied for very poor ratings, assuming the parent has the skill to implement these kinds of consequences in a calm and not overly punitive fashion.

6. After the parent has agreed to the procedure, have the child join you and the parent. Describe your concerns to the child and the idea of using a daily report card. Involve the student in generating a menu of potential home rewards. You can give him a copy of the list of rewards in this book. Set realistic criteria for earning a daily reward at home. As with other reward programs, the goals should be well within the reach of the child. If possible, you may also wish to include rewards at school.

7. Finalize the daily report card and procedures. Establish the responsibilities of all parties involved. Teachers are typically responsible for completing the card and signing it. Students are typically responsible for handing the card to

the teacher for signing at an appropriate time (e.g., end of class), taking it home and showing it to parents. Parents are typically responsible for delivering rewards if earned or withholding rewards if not earned. Have the student go through a "practice day" to make sure he or she understands the program. The student should be able to describe the specific target behaviors, the criteria, and the way the ratings on the card translate into rewards at home. Also make sure that the student has a place to carry the report card between school and home. Make up a contract with the responsibilities of all parties and signatures.

8. Troubleshoot the following potential problems with parent and student::

- What happens when the student forgets the card? Answer: The day is treated as if the goal was not achieved. This means the parent withholds the reward.

- What happens when the student claims the teacher did not have time or refused to sign the card? Answer: The day is treated as if the goal was not achieved. Assure the parent that you will be available to sign the card. But be sure the student knows when to ask you.

- What happens in the case of forgery or tampering? At a minimum, the day is treated as if the goal was not achieved. The parent may also wish to withhold an additional privilege, or write an apology note to the teacher for forging.

- What happens when the schedule is changed or there is a substitute? Usually the program is not in effect when a substitute teacher is present. However, the student is still responsible for his or her behavior and if any negative reports come home, rewards would be withheld, or consequences levied.

9. Start the program and follow through:

- Make copies of the daily report card. It is often useful to have the par-

ent and child create the report cards at home. However, the program is often expedited if you make the copies.

- Initially, provide student with prompts for success. Remind the student to give you the card and throughout the day notice the student's progress and comment on how well he or she is doing toward meeting the daily goal.

- Be positive. Encourage parents to focus on what their child did well each day. If problems occur, have parents ask their child what he or she might do to improve the next day.

- Be consistent.

10. Schedule a follow-up contact for one to two weeks after the initial meeting to check on the progress of the program. If all is well, this contact may be via a note to the parent or a telephone call. If problems are continuing or if the card doesn't seem to be implemented as planned, try to schedule another meeting or telephone contact. These programs often need some modification.

On the following page is a list of activities, privileges, and tangible rewards that parents may wish to use at home to reward the child for meeting daily, weekly, or longer-term goals.

Remember that the most effective report cards are those where target goals are very specific (e.g., no more than three interruptions, at least four assignments completed) so that it is very clear what you want the child to do. Report cards that use very general, evaluative goals (e.g., be a good student) with feedback given only at the end of the day (or week) often don't work. The child should get feedback at least several times a day. For one particularly difficult student, Mary Olvak set up a report card with the initial goal being no more than six interruptions per half hour. As the student was able to do this, the goal was increased, so that over several months, the student was able to be successful with a goal set at no more than one interruption per half-hour period. At first, Ms. Olvak found monitoring the student's behavior every 15-30 minutes to be somewhat overwhelming. But

she says that it didn't take long for her to find this procedure to be "absolutely easier" than constantly dealing with negative behavior. She also says that using this approach helped reduce her anger, since the focus is on giving the student factual feedback about his or her behavior (e.g., "that's more than 3 interruptions, no points for this period"), and not on winning a battle with the student.

Handling parent questions and concerns

Parent: I'm sure Kevin would like to earn some of these things. But don't you think he should be able to do his work without them? I'm worried that he'll only do the work for the reward.

Teacher: I understand your concern. But all kids need rewards. Right now, Kevin does not seem to be responding to the rewards in class that some of the other kids respond to, like getting good grades. This program would simply involve adding an extra incentive to make it very clear that doing well in school pays off. At the beginning, he may work primarily for the rewards, but over time, he should begin enjoying the satisfaction of doing a good job and getting good grades.

Parent: I don't get home until 7:00 every night and I don't have much time to reward my child.

Teacher: Effective rewards often don't have to take much time. Consider a bedtime story or a 10-minute game with you. I have a feeling your child would really value this time with you even if it's only 10 minutes. It could make a big difference in his work at school.

Parent: I'm worried that my son will feel embarrassed or singled out with this report card.

Teacher: It may be hard for your son not to feel somewhat singled out. But this approach is meant to help him be more successful in school, which should help improve how he feels about himself. Also, we can make the report card as private as possible. He can come up at the end of class to get

my signature or leave it for me at the beginning of the class and pick it up at the end. As he shows improvement, he can work his way off the contract.

Parent: What should I do if my son brings home a report card showing he had a bad day and didn't earn very many points?

Teacher: When your son brings home such a report, you might try asking him in a calm way about what did not go so well. But don't get into a long discussion about the problem. If your son refuses to take responsibility for the problem, don't keep pressing him to get a "confession." Just let it go. It's usually better not to dwell on the problem but focus more on how he can improve—ask him what he could work on to do better the next day. Also, don't overlook those things that did go well. Whatever you do, be sure that your son does not get the reward he would have gotten if the report was a good one. Don't argue with your son over this or let him talk you out of it! The next morning, give him encouragement to have a good day. If you have any questions about what happened, feel free to contact me.

List of suggested home rewards:

Daily

Back massage
Bedtime story
Bubble bath
Chore pass
Computer time
Food or drink treat after school
Game with parent
Helping to cook
Later bedtime
Money
Outside play
Playing with friends
Practice sport with parent
Ride bike
Rollerblading
Snack of choice
Special dessert
Swimming
Telephone privileges
Trip to park
TV time

Weekly

Arts/crafts
Buy new cassette tape or CD
Cooking
Eating out at restaurant
Getting a new book
Go bowling
Going somewhere alone with
  parent
Going to beach or lake
Going to video arcade
Grab bag
Hair clips
Outing to spend money earned
Overnight with friend
Rental movie
Trip to mall

Monthly or Longer

Amusement park
New clothes
Sporting goods

Chapter Five

Deciding Which Procedures to Use

You've identified the problems and you're aware of the many options you have for dealing with the problems. How do you know what to do and when to do it? Here are some guidelines:

1. Start first with "low-cost," good teaching strategies (see Chapter Two of this book).

2. Select a solution relevant to the problem at hand based on your assessment of what's setting it off and what's maintaining the problem. For example, if being around certain peers sets off the problem, consider moving the student's seat. If the student is bored and easily distracted during lessons, involve the student more often in the lesson. If the student misbehaves to get your attention, give attention to the student, but only when he or she is behaving well!

3. Don't just try to reduce problem behaviors. Always replace negative behaviors with positive ones.

4. Set up reward programs before using punishment.

5. Use developmentally appropriate strategies. Younger children usually need more frequent feedback, concrete rewards given right away, more prompting, and very

simple, brief directions. Older children can manage with a somewhat greater delay in receiving rewards and less frequent feedback (but not a lot less). They should be more actively involved in designing the program and take more responsibility for it including monitoring their own behavior. They often respond well to contracts.

6. Decide what to do based on what's practical for you. Ms. Kelly Passante found that strategies she could implement fairly easily into her daily routine had the best chance for working. Complicated programs were prone to inconsistency. She advises teachers that if something is too hard or complicated, think about how you can simplify it to meet your needs as well as the needs of the student. Strategies need to be individualized for teachers just as they are for students!

7. Think of interventions as "mini-experiments." Sometimes it is hard to know if something will work without trying it. Decide on an intervention, and then see what effect it has. If improvement does not occur, begin another experiment with another intervention.

The checklist that follows summarizes many of the strategies presented in this book and can be used as a guide to select solutions. The strategies are divided into ten general areas with sample problems relevant to each. However, keep in mind that most of the strategies are useful for many different problems. Likewise, many problems benefit from strategies in a combination of different areas. Refer to related book sections for more specific information about particular strategies.

Strategies Checklist

Area 1. Arrange the classroom environment to promote learning readiness.

Problem: Is the student's problem behavior set off by peers? Is the student easily distracted?

❑ Have student sit near the front of the class, away from distractions, by positive peer role models.

❑ Keep classroom uncluttered and well-organized.

❑ Utilize visual aides to emphasize limits and rules.

Area 2. Use interactive teaching styles and techniques.

Problem: Does the student seem bored or quickly lose interest in things? Is the student more interested in his peers or the contents of his desk than in listening to your lecture? Is the student unable to sustain the attention necessary to finish work?

❑ Actively involve students in lessons.

❑ Use high interest, multisensory, and hands-on approaches.

❑ Have well-organized lesson plans.

❑ Pace lectures for ability and attention span (shorten, limit down time).

❑ Frequently move around class when lecturing or monitoring independent seatwork to allow for scanning and feedback.

❑ Provide immediate feedback regarding quality of work produced.

Area 3. Give tools to improve organizational skills.

Problem: Does the student fail to complete assignments? Does the student always seem to be losing things? Does the student often fail to get the right assignment?

❑ Use daily assignment books.

❑ Use written descriptions of daily and long-term assignments.

❑ Use color-coded activities and assignment folders.

❑ Use folder taped to the side of desk for completed
   papers.

❑ Organize student desk/work space, have desk checks.

❑ Assign study buddy.

Area 4. Make accommodations to assignments.

Problem: Does the student seem overwhelmed by lengthy assignments?
Does the student seem to get tired easily when doing tasks that require a lot
of mental effort? Does the student seem to take longer to complete work
than other students in your class?

❑ Shorten assignments.

❑ Allow use of word processors, spelling checks, etc.

❑ Allot extra time to complete tests, assignments.

❑ Provide brief work breaks.

❑ Break tasks into manageable, small parts.

❑ Use student-selected projects in areas of interest.

Area 5. Use these guidelines for class rules:

Problem: Does the student seem to "forget" class rules? Are the rules hard
to follow or hard to remember?

❑ Keep rules simple; add new rules if needed.

❑ Generate rules with student input.

❑ Post rules in the front of the class.

❑ Use hand signs or other nonverbal prompts to remind kids of rules.

❑ State consequences for following and not following rules.

Area 6. Use these guidelines for giving directions:

Problem: Do you often have to repeat your directions many times? Does the student often fail to follow your directions? Does the student not seem to understand your directions?

❑ Use statements (e.g., "You have a direction to..."), not questions.

❑ Give only one direction at a time.

❑ Be specific and brief.

❑ Give in a neutral or positive tone of voice.

❑ Have student repeat direction to ensure understanding.

Area 7. Use positive attention.

Problem: Do you want the student to be doing more of something? (e.g., more work, more listening, more following directions)

❑ Make it strategic: praise those behaviors you want to see more often.

❑ Acknowledge good behavior immediately.

❑ Make praise specific.

❑ Be genuine.

❑ Praise often.

Area 8. Use rewards and incentives.

Problem: Do you want the student to be doing more of something and positive attention is not enough?

❑ Use privileges and activities as rewards at more frequent intervals.

❏ Add individual, class-wide, or group rewards.

❏ Use token economies with short and long-term rewards.

❏ Have students pick own rewards.

❏ Use reward menus; change rewards frequently.

❏ Set realistic goals.

❏ Have student self-monitor and evaluate their own behavior.

❏ Draw up a contract with the student.

Area 9. Use prudent negative consequences.

Problem: Do you want the student to stop a behavior? (e.g., stop interrupting, stop talking, stop fighting, stop fooling around)

❏ Catch problem behavior as soon as it starts.

❏ Be very brief, use only a few words.

❏ Stay calm and matter-of-fact.

❏ Don't use more than one warning.

❏ Give feedback privately to the student.

❏ Use response cost, work tasks, or time-out.

❏ Don't rely on negative consequences alone.

Area 10. Involve parents.

Problem: Are the student's problems repetitive or of major significance? Is the student failing to turn in homework? Are classroom-based rewards and negative consequences not enough?

❏ Contact parents early on.

❏ Promote a team spirit.

❏ Use a daily school-home report card with consequences at home.

❏ Make homework expectations explicit.

Putting It All Together: Sample Solutions to Common Problems of ADHD Students

See how the strategies checklist is used to handle eight common problems. Next to each problem are the numbers of the strategy areas on the checklist that were used to solve the problem.

Problem 1: Starting and stopping tasks/activities on time.

Areas: 1, 2, 3, 4, 6, 7

Ryan, a fourth grader, had great difficulty getting started on his assignments. He often couldn't seem to find the right page in the book, or the materials he needed. Then, once started, he had trouble stopping when he was told to and switching to another activity.

Solution: His teacher decided to move his seat to the front where she could assist him during transitions. She made a point of making sure he understood the instructions by having him repeat them back to her. She praised him for accuracy. She also decided to use a check-off card which included the steps he needed to follow to start a task (Get the right book, find the right page, get pencil and paper, do the first problem, or read the first paragraph). Ryan would check off each step as it was completed. She praised him for using the card and getting started on his work. To help him stop activities, she gave him advance warning and clear specific directions. She also gave extra praise for stopping when told to stop.

Problem 2: Disruptions: Calling out, interrupting, making too much noise

Areas: 1,5,7,8,9

Justin, a second grader, was very loud and impulsive in class. He often blurted out during class discussions. He bothered his neighbors during independent seat work by whispering or making noises.

Solution: Justin's teacher decided to move his seat away from peers who were likely to interact with him at the wrong times. He also established a class rule for handraising and posted it on the wall. Whenever he saw Justin following the rule, he praised him (as he did other children following the rule). These changes helped, but Justin continued to call out in class. So, his teacher decided to use a response cost/token program. The token was a card with 3 pictures of a raised hand. He gave Justin a "token" card for every period (there were 6 periods during the day). Every time he called out, the teacher crossed out a hand. At the end of the day, Justin counted the number of hands left on his card. For every hand left, he could earn one minute of time on the computer.

Problem 3: Not attending to lectures and class discussions

Areas: 2, 7, 8

Scott, a fifth grader, routinely daydreamed during class. His teacher noticed that even though he was seated near the front, he seemed to drift off into his own world. He seldom asked questions or participated in class discussions. The teacher was also concerned that the whole class was starting to tune-out lectures.

Solution: Scott's teacher decided to change some things to improve the attention and participation of all the students. He began making discussions more

interesting for everyone by using relevant examples and more hands-on activities. He frequently repeated what he said to make sure everyone heard. He prompted students to pay attention and participate by implementing a class-wide reward program in which all students earned points for participating in class discussions and answering "attention checks" accurately. Attention checks involved asking students impromptu questions about the material being discussed. To make sure all students were called on, the teacher made up a deck of cards with each student's name on a card. He randomly pulled a card from the deck to determine who would be asked each attention check. Because Scott had particular difficulty attending, he made sure to call on Scott at a more frequent rate than the other students. Points were accumulated every day and earnings were publicly posted on a chart in the room. After the chart was filled up (this took several weeks) the class earned a popcorn party.

The teacher also did several things specifically to help Scott. He told Scott in advance that he would be called on during group lessons. He also increased his involvement in the lesson by having Scott keep track of participation points earned during discussions, using Scott's work as a sample for the whole class and having Scott demonstrate principles related to the lecture (with help as needed).

Problem 4: Not completing work

Areas: 3, 4, 7, 8, 10

Lisa, a third grader, seldom completed assigned work. She seemed to understand the concepts, but it took great effort on her part to stay focused. She often became frustrated when she did not complete the work on time and would give up. She seemed to be losing interest in school.

Solution: Lisa's teacher took a two-pronged approach to the problem. First, she made accommodations to the assignments and second, she set

up a daily school-home contract with completed work as the target behavior. Lisa earned a point for all assignments completed accurately and neatly. She used a timer to help Lisa complete assignments more quickly. She set the timer at the beginning of independent seat work. If Lisa "beat the clock" she was able to earn bonus points on her school-home contract. The teacher reduced the quantity of repetitive work, but told Lisa that she could earn extra bonus points for completing more than the modified assignment. Lisa was also given extra time to complete her work. Lisa exchanged her points for daily rewards (TV time) and weekly rewards (eating out) at home.

Problem 5: Defiant, aggressive behavior

Areas: 5, 6, 7, 8, 9

David, a first grader, was extremely defiant during class. He refused to follow teacher directions and made rude remarks under his breath. He teased his classmates and would push or hit them if they got in his way.

Solution: David's teacher decided to do several things. First, she clarified that a class rule prohibited hitting and saying mean things. She made sure to catch David when he was getting along with peers and following her directions. She praised him and reminded him that he was working toward being able to earn recess and free time because he was showing self-control. She also established time-out and work tasks as consequences for hitting or pushing. Whenever David was aggressive he would get a ten minute time-out in the back of the class. If he went right away, that amount was reduced to two minutes. If he didn't go to time-out, he also had to do ten tasks. Each task involved him drawing a diagonal line through a small box. Tasks not completed during class were completed after school.

Problem 6: Not following directions

Areas: 6, 7, 8

Maya, a fourth grader, often failed to follow teacher instructions to sit down, stop talking to her neighbor, put her book away, line up, etc. She wasn't defiant; she simply didn't seem to hear the instruction or seemed to forget it right after she heard it. She was easily distracted by other things, which didn't help matters.

Solution: Maya's teacher decided to change the way she gave directions. She stopped giving directions by asking questions and made her directions very clear, brief, specific, and only gave one at a time. She began having Maya repeat the direction to make sure she understood. She praised Maya when she followed directions right away. (She found that praising her as she started to comply often prompted her to finish complying!) Just changing the way she gave instructions seemed to help, but she decided to start a group reward program to help all students follow directions right away. She divided the class into six teams corresponding to the six rows of students. She gave out row points for those rows who followed directions right away. Row points were totaled every day. Rows with the most points earned privileges the next day (lining up first). Row points were also accumulated for a class party.

Problem 7: Low frustration tolerance

Areas: 6, 7, 8, 10

Mark, a second grader, easily became upset whenever something did not go the way he wanted it to go. Any disappointment would trigger a tantrum.

Solution: Mark's teacher began a program to help Mark learn to tolerate disappointments. He told Mark that he was going to look for situations that often made Mark frustrated like getting called out in a game, not being chosen for an activity, having to wait to get help from the teacher when he was busy, and not being able to do a certain activity on a given day. When he saw that Mark was accepting a situation he didn't like without crying, complaining, or tantrumming, he was going to praise him and give him a point for accepting on his school-home report card. To help him out, the teacher

would also try to prompt Mark with a direction to show accepting right before a potential disappointment.

Problem 8: Transition problems

Area: 3

Erik, a sixth grader, was very disorganized. He seldom retrieved or put away his books, pencils, paper, and other materials in a timely fashion, and he seemed to always be losing his things.

Solution: Erik's teacher assigned Erik a study buddy. The buddy was a classmate who was chosen because he was mild-mannered and well-organized. Before each period, the teacher would tell both boys to get the materials they needed together. At the end of each period, they would  put their books and materials away together. The study buddy served as a model for how to handle materials and keep organized during transitions.

Chapter Six

Evaluating Whether the Program Is Working

How do you know if the program is working? The obvious answer is that the program is working if the problem behavior is decreased and some alternative acceptable behavior is in its place. Many teachers have a sense of this, but accurate, objective records of the child's behavior are necessary to know for sure. The best way to track progress is by keeping daily charts or logs of the student's performance. If a token system is used, this may simply be the number of tokens earned per day.

If behavior is improving and the program seems to be working, keep it up for at least two to three weeks without changing it. Then if success continues, you can begin to make modifications to expand the program, further shape behavior to your eventual goal, or even begin fading the program.

How to Sink Your Own Ship

If the program is not working, identify the reasons for its failure. Without realizing it, teachers are sometimes their own worst enemies in the classroom. Many of the approaches recommended here can be rendered ineffective by

common teaching mistakes. When this happens, the teacher may be incorrectly convinced that the techniques don't work, and then abandon tools that could have helped them be more successful in teaching. Below is a list of suggestions that will keep you from undermining your effectiveness:

How to Have an Effective Program

1. Don't argue back. DO NOT let yourself be drawn into an argument or discussion of your rules or whether or not the student was following them. State the facts and give your interventions without responding to protests.

2. Don't give unnecessary explanations. In most cases, it is unnecessary to provide a rationale for your commands or rules. Giving rationales often only invites argu ments or causes the student to focus on the rationale rather than on the command.

3. Don't yell. It is often more effective to lower your voice when redirecting a student. Displays of emotion (anger, exasperation) can be rewarding for many students.

4. Don't take good behavior for granted.

5. Don't follow rewards with a negative comment (e.g., "Why can't you do this all the time?).

6. Don't give half-hearted praise in a tone suggesting that you don't mean it.

7. Don't criticize or humiliate the student in front of the class.

8. Don't give in and let the student have the reward before he or she earned it.

9. Don't give in and let the student have the reward when they plead or throw tantrums.

10. Don't give too many second chances.

11. Don't forget about the program or forget to complete the daily report card.

12. Don't expect too much or set the standards for reward too high for an individual ADHD student.

13. Don't expect too little.

14. Don't give up once the student loses interest in the reward. Know in advance that your reward program will work for a while and then lose its effectiveness. Modify the program, do not abandon it.

Common Reasons for Program Failure:

1. Target behavior is vague. *("Be a good student.")*

2. Consequences are not immediate enough. *(Only a weekly reward is given.)*

3. Student was never interested in the reward. *(Not all kids like candy.)*

4. Student does not mind the negative consequence. *(Some students don't like recess anyway.)*

5. Peers are reinforcing the negative behavior. *(Getting a classmate to laugh at silly behavior is a powerful reinforcer.)*

6. Other factors reinforce the negative behavior. *(A student throws a tantrum in class and gets out of doing the work.)*

7. Program is not practical to do. *(too many target behaviors, too complicated.)*

8. Parents undermine the program. *(Parents don't agree with the teacher's concerns)*

9. Parents don't follow through with home consequences. *(Parents are too busy to give rewards at home.)*

10. Program is not clear to the student. *(Student could not describe her own program accurately.)*

Apply Problem-Solving to Modify the Program

Follow these steps:

- First, make a list of some reasons why the program may not be working.

- Next, brainstorm some solutions.

- Then, select those solutions most likely to help the problem.

- Implement the changes and evaluate. Did the changes fix the problem? If not, are there other solutions to try?

Example 1: Remember Maya in the previous example. She had trouble following directions promptly. At first she responded well to the teacher chang-

ing the way she gave commands and the row points. But after a few weeks, she began not following directions again.

First, make a list of some reasons why the program may not be working.

- Maya lost interest in the reward of a class party.

- The reward may be too far in the future.

- I've stopped having her repeat the direction after I give it.

Next, brainstorm some solutions.

- Change the group reward.

- Use an individual reward in addition to the group reward.

- Make the reward more immediate.

- Continue having her repeat the direction.

Then, select those solutions most likely to help the problem.

- Add an individual daily reward for Maya on days she follows most directions right away. The reward will be given by Maya's parents at home through use of a daily report card.

- Have her repeat the directions again.

Implement the changes and evaluate. Did the changes fix the problem? If not are there other solutions to try?

- Maya started following directions again. I'll plan to re-evaluate the program in two weeks to see if additional changes are needed.

Example 2: David, the defiant and aggressive student did not seem to be responding to the punishment of time-out and work tasks. He was receiving five to six time-outs per day.

First, make a list of some reasons why the program may not be working:

- I'm not staying very calm when he defies me and he seems to be successful at getting me to argue with him about his behavior.

- I might be giving him too many warnings before sending him to time-out.

- These problems may be making time-out less of a punishment.

- The praise I'm giving may not be a powerful enough reinforcer.

Next, brainstorm some solutions:

- Stay calm and avoid arguments at all cost!

- Have him go to time-out right away. No second chances.

- Give him lots of praise when he follows my directions.

- Let him earn stickers if he doesn't have more than one time-out a day.

Then, select those solutions most likely to help the problem:

- All of the above.

Implement changes and evaluate.

- It worked! David stopped being so defiant and seemed to like earning the stickers.

Remember: most programs will require some modification initially and over time to be successful. The need for change does not mean behavioral programs are not effective. It is simply part of what makes them work.

Chapter Seven

ADHD: Beyond the Classroom

A Brief History of ADHD

Over the years, many labels have been applied to children having ADHD. In 1902, George Still first described children who were inattentive, defiant, overly emotional, and uninhibited as having "deficits in moral control." Later, such children were provided with the label Minimal Brain Dysfunction. With increased recognition that these kids did not have gross brain abnormalities (or control deficits related to moral issues), the name changed to Hyperkinetic Disorder of Childhood in the second version of the Diagnostic and Statistical Manual for Mental Disorders (DSM). This manual, published by the American Psychiatric Association, is the one used by psychiatrists, psychologists, and other mental health practitioners across the country to identify the full range of child and adult mental health disorders. It is revised every few years to reflect changes in our understanding of these disorders based on research studies. In 1980, the third revision of the DSM was published and the label of ADD was provided. This term reflected the prevailing view that inattention, not hyperactivity, was the primary problem. The term ADHD was first used in 1987 with the revised version of the third

edition of the DSM. This term has continued into the recently published fourth version of the DSM (1994), but now there are three subtypes: primarily inattentive, primarily hyperactive impulsive, and combined (both inattentive and hyperactive impulsive) reflecting the extent to which the two core symptom areas are present.

How is ADD/ADHD identified?

Who Can Diagnose ADHD?

ADHD is not an easy disorder to diagnose. All of the symptoms are characteristic of normal childhood so it becomes critical to discriminate the disorder from normal child development. It is equally important to discriminate ADHD from other disorders, since symptoms of other disorders can often look like ADHD. Because of the diagnostic complications, it is imperative that the diagnostic evaluation be conducted by a professional well-trained in psychiatric diagnoses, child psychopathology, normal child development, and psychometrics. Usually a clinical psychologist, child psychiatrist or behavioral pediatrician with expertise in ADD/ADHD, disruptive behavior, and emotional problems has the training and background to provide a diagnostic evaluation. There is also a growing trend to provide school psychologists with the skills needed for assessing ADHD.

The Diagnostic Criteria for ADHD:

The psychiatric diagnosis of ADHD is made using the criteria outlined in the Diagnostic and Statistical Manual for Mental Disorders (DSM-IV). To meet criteria for ADHD, at least six of the symptoms in one of the following two groupings must have been present for at least six months to a degree that is maladaptive and inconsistent with developmental level:

Problems with inattention:

a) often fails to give close attention to details or makes careless mistakes in schoolwork, work, or other activities

b) often has difficulty sustaining attention in tasks or play activities

c) often does not seem to listen when spoken to directly

d) often does not follow through on instructions and fails to finish schoolwork, chores, or duties in the workplace

e) often has difficulty organizing tasks and activities

f) often avoids, dislikes, or is reluctant to engage in tasks that require sustained mental effort (such as schoolwork or homework)

g) often loses things necessary for tasks or activities (e.g., toys, school assignments, pencils, books, or tools)

h) is often easily distracted by extraneous stimuli; is often forgetful in daily activities

Problems with hyperactivity or impulsivity:

a) often fidgets with hands or feet and squirms in seat

b) often leaves seat in classroom or in other situations in which remaining seated is expected

c) often runs about or climbs excessively in situations in which it is inappropriate

d) often has difficulty playing or engaging in leisure activities quietly

e) is often "on the go" or often acts as if "driven by a motor"

f) often talks excessively

g) often blurts out answers before questions have been completed

h) often has difficulty awaiting turn

i) often interrupts or intrudes on others

In addition, the symptoms need to have been present since before the child turned seven years old and must cause social or academic impairment in at least two settings (e.g., at home and school).

Subtypes of ADHD:

ADHD-Predominantly Inattentive Type: High on inattention (6 or more from the list of 9 inattention symptoms) and low on hyperactive-impulsive (less than 6 hyperactive-impulsive symptoms).

ADHD-Predominantly Hyperactive-Impulsive Type: Low on inattention (less than 6 inattention symptoms) and high on hyperactive-impulsive (6 or more hyperactive-impulsive symptoms).

ADHD-Combined Type: High on inattention (6 or more inattention symptoms) and high on hyperactive-impulsive (6 or more hyperactive-impulsive symptoms).

What Should You Do if You Suspect that a Student may have ADHD?

As a teacher, you may be one of the first to notice a child's extreme inattention, impulsivity, or overactivity in a structured setting. Parents have often observed difficulty at home, but in many cases, problems are more obvious in school.

As a first step you should collect information regarding the student's academic work and behavior in class. Be specific about your concerns; this information will be useful in communicating with parents and other school personnel.

Next, consult with or make a referral to the school psychologist, guidance counselor, special education teacher, principal or other school personnel with expertise in ADHD or attention/behavior problems. Have a specialist in handling these problems informally observe the student in your class. A referral for a formal assessment may be needed to evaluate ADHD-related

concerns. If so, you should be aware of your school's policy for making referrals to evaluate the need for special services. There are several mechanisms to obtain services for ADHD students (see page 25), and very specific legal guidelines usually need to be followed. Remember that the diagnosis of ADHD requires special training and experience and will need to be made by a professional who specializes in assessing and treating ADHD.

You don't need to wait for the results of the evaluation to begin implementing interventions in the classroom. Share your concerns about specific problems with the parents. You may wish to start a school-home intervention or make additional accommodations for the student in class immediately. Keep records of the student's response to these interventions, including all work samples and behavior records. These records are important for gauging the student's progress and determining the need for additional intervention. They will also be helpful in the event that a student study team meeting takes place.

What Are the Roles of Professionals in Making a Diagnosis and Providing Treatment?

A number of different professionals are usually involved in evaluating and treating ADHD. School personnel, psychologists, physicians, outside professionals, and parents need to work together as part of a team. Clear communication among everyone is essential.

Teacher's role: As a part of the evaluation, you will likely be called upon to give a detailed description of the student's academic progress, behavior, and social relations in class and to complete a series of standard behavior rating scales. Your input to the diagnostic process is critical. School is very often the place in which children have the most difficulty. You are in the best position to provide information about the child's behavior at school. Take the time to be

accurate. In addition to providing information for the evaluation, don't be hesitant about asking questions of the team. Get their ideas for working with the ADHD child in class.

Role of psychologist: A clinical psychologist with expertise in working with ADHD can provide the evaluation. The psychologist often serves as the case coordinator, gathering information from all sources, and integrating the data to formulate diagnostic impressions and make recommendations. The psychologist usually interviews the parents to assess the child's development, history of problems and current symptoms. The psychologist also interviews the teacher (if possible) and child. Psychologists interpret behavior rating scales and checklists completed by parents and teachers and review school records. Psychologists also administer intelligence and achievement tests (supplemented with neuropsychological tests, if necessary) to evaluate for possible learning disabilities. At the end of the evaluation, diagnostic impressions are provided by the psychologist, usually in the form of a written report, and recommendations for further evaluation or treatment are made. Psychologists may provide treatments such as parent training, family therapy, and social skills training. They may also consult with teachers and parents about setting up coordinated school-home programs.

Role of physician: A child psychiatrist or behavioral pediatrician can also provide an evaluation for ADHD. The physician performs a medical and developmental history and obtains information from parents and children about current functioning and symptoms. They complete physical and neurological exams to assess for medical problems that may accompany ADHD; however, these exams are not necessary for a diagnosis of ADHD. Physicians may also use standardized parent and teacher ratings of behavior. Unlike psychologists, physicians do not usually administer cognitive tests such as IQ and achievement tests. Physicians provide recommendations for treatment following the evaluation. Physicians often recommend the use of medication to treat ADHD. Physicians, but not psychologists can prescribe medication.

Role of school psychologist: School psychologists with expertise in ADHD may provide many of the same procedures as a clinical psychologist. An advantage they have is the ability to observe the child directly during class. This is usually impractical for an outside professional to do. The school psychologist plays a key role in facilitating the initial evaluation and setting up a student study meeting where all school personnel, outside professionals, and the child's parents can meet about the student's educational needs, the possibility of special education, and setting up necessary interventions for the student at school. Many school psychologists also have training in working with ADHD students in class and can make recommendations for accommodations and management plans in the classroom.

Role of school administration: The role of the administrative staff is one of setting the stage so that quality education can happen. Effective administrators encourage training in methods for working with ADHD students and provide opportunities for in-services on ADHD. They know that working with ADHD students can be extremely challenging and demoralizing for any teacher. They do their best to provide necessary support staff, materials, and supplies and they attend student study team meetings. They recognize the efforts of their teachers and routinely offer support.

Educational Identification and Policies Relevant for ADHD

During recent years, educational policy regarding ADHD has been at the forefront of debate at the federal, state, and district level. As more is known of the disorder, as more organized parent advocacy groups have formed, and as more educators have become familiar with the range of handicaps these children exhibit in class, policy has been clarified and shaped to offer more services to meet the needs of these children than ever before. At this time, two mechanisms exist for ADHD children to qualify for special services. These two mechanisms include: the "Other Health Impaired" category of Part B of the Individuals with Disabilities Act (IDEA), and Section 504 of the Rehabilitation Act of 1973. The U.S. Department of Education has

indicated that both of these policies dictate that individuals with an attention deficit disorder that causes impairment in educational performance are eligible for special education or related services. Services may include accommodations in the regular classroom, a resource program for part of the day, or a full-day, self-contained special education classroom.

School policy regarding methods for identifying ADHD and methods for documenting the need for special services is currently being decided in many districts. Historically, the diagnosis of ADHD has usually been farmed out to physicians and psychologists in the community. This practice may decrease as school psychologists obtain expertise in ADHD and training in diagnostic and assessment methods. State-of-the-art methods for assessing ADHD include: review of birth, developmental and medical history, review of school records, completion of standardized rating scales by parents and teachers, symptom-related interviews administered to parents and teachers (if possible), review of social and emotional functioning, and intelligence and achievement testing to assess for learning problems. The need for special education services requires documentation of academic impairment in addition to a diagnosis of ADHD. Achievement tests are usually not sensitive for picking up such impairment. Instead, failure to complete assigned work (with accuracy) on a regular basis, or school records showing impaired study skills, disorganization or other academic problems may be used to assess impairment. Not all ADHD students will qualify for special services, since some may not be exhibiting educational impairment. For those who do qualify, the type of services should be tailored to the severity of the problems. Many ADHD students will perform quite well with accommodations to the regular classroom; others with more severe difficulties may require placement in more restrictive settings.

What Are the Treatments for ADHD?

The focus of this book has been on the treatment most important for educators: classroom accommodations and behavior management strategies. Use

of these strategies is recommended for virtually all ADHD students. Additional treatments, however, are usually necessary to obtain the most successful outcomes. Medication is perhaps the most widely used treatment and in combination with behavioral approaches, is considered to be the most potent treatment for ADHD (Pelham & Murphy, 1996). The use of medication is discussed below. For ADHD-like problems at home, parent training or behavioral family therapy are the treatments of choice. These treatments help parents learn how to manage their children's attention and behavior and have been shown to be effective for ADHD children in many research studies. Group-based behavioral therapies such as social skills training can assist in improving peer-related problems. Individual therapies can be useful for dealing with emotional problems, but are not effective for treating ADHD per se. Educational therapy is recommended for ADHD children with learning disabilities. A number of other treatments have been touted as being effective with ADHD children, but insufficient research data supports their use. Although no known treatment cures ADHD, behavioral interventions (in school and at home), often in combination with medication, can lead to dramatic improvement in overall functioning.

What Teachers Should Know about Medication Treatment

Medication therapy is probably the most common form of intervention for ADHD children. Psychostimulant medications such as Ritalin (methylphenidate), Dexedrine (dextroamphetamine), and Cylert (pemoline) are the most widely used medicines to treat ADHD. As many as 70 to 80% of children having ADHD respond positively to stimulant medication (Swanson, McBurnett, Christian & Wigal, 1995). This usually means that when they take the medication they are able to focus their attention for longer periods of time, are less active and impulsive, are more compliant, get more of their work done, and get along better with others (teachers, parents, and other children). ADHD children with or without hyperactivity show positive effects from medication in the short-term, but there is no evi-

dence yet of long-term positive effects of medication use (Swanson, McBurnett, Wigal, Pfiffner, Christian, Tamm, Willcutt, Crowley, Clevenger, & Woo (1993).

Psychostimulant medication is thought to work by modulating arousal in the parts of the brain that control attention, inhibition, and activity level. However, the mechanism(s) accounting for the clinical effects are not clearly understood (Swanson et al, 1995). Some people used to think that the medication had a paradoxical effect on ADHD children. But research studies show that stimulant medication seems to work the same way with both normal and ADHD children (Swanson et al, 1995). Most stimulant medications work for relatively short periods of time (usually about three to four hours), so multiple doses in a day are usually required. Some medications can work for up to eight hours (Cylert, sustained-release versions of Ritalin, or Dexedrine spansules), although there is wide variation among children. Some children do not respond well to stimulants or have other problems in addition to ADHD. For these children, another class of medications called antidepressants might be used.

It is hard to predict who will respond well to medication and to what type and at what dose. This needs to be determined for each child. A consultation with a physician is required and a medication trial is often done. The trial usually involves carefully monitoring a child's response to various dosages to determine the optimal level (see, for example, Gadow, 1993).

What is the Teacher's Role?

Medication is prescribed mostly for school-related problems. Therefore, your role in communicating with parents and physicians is a critical one. First of all, teachers should provide information to the student's parents and physician about the student's behavioral, social, and academic performance in school prior to medication use. This kind of information is important as baseline data. It will be the standard against which the effects of medication will be measured.

After the child begins medication, you will be in the position to monitor the effects. Be prepared to provide feedback about the student's progress to the parents and physician. Some districts have standard reporting formats to use, such as rating scales and questionnaires. You should look for possible positive changes in the child's behavior, such as increased attention span and compliance, decreased impulsivity and physical activity, and increased work  productivity. You should also look for possible negative effects. Some children show improved behavior, but become over focused and glassy-eyed on medication. Often this means that the dose is too high. Side effects are also common. These might include insomnia, appetite suppression, headaches, stomachaches, or increased motor or verbal tics. Some children also have mood swings or greater irritability, especially when the medication is wearing off. This information is important for the physician in determining the appropriateness of medication and the optimal type and dose.

After the best dose has been determined, keep monitoring the child. Communicate any changes in behavior or performance to the parents and physician. Sometimes adjustments in the type or dose of medication are necessary after a period of time.

Keep in mind that medication is only one tool for improving ADHD students' performance. Medication is not recommended as the sole treatment for ADHD. Other treatments such as classroom interventions and parent training are usually necessary.

Chapter Eight

Energizing and Re-energizing for Teachers

1. Being around ADHD students can be exhausting. Implementing a consistent behavior modification program with ADHD students is a tough job. Don't neglect your own emotional needs. Don't count on the students to meet all of your needs. Make sure you have outlets for re-energizing: Exercise regularly, talk to friends, consult with colleagues, take a break before you see your own kids, etc. Remember to get plenty of sleep and don't lose your sense of humor!

2. Set small goals for yourself and reward yourself every step of the way. Take one day at a time. Treat yourself for remembering to catch good behavior or staying calm during an outburst. Give yourself a special treat for taking the extra time needed to be consistent.

3. Get help from other professionals. No one has all the answers. Sometimes it's easier for a person not so involved in the situation to look at

the student objectively. Set up a support system with other teachers to help keep you motivated and consistent. Give each other daily support for following through and coping with difficult behaviors.

4. Expect that you will have "bad" days. You may find that you have slipped out of the habits of good behavior management. Encourage yourself to "get back on the wagon" and not give up. Don't let yourself get trapped by feelings of guilt or inadequacy. It's OK to make mistakes.

5. Expect that ADHD students will have setbacks. They may inexplicably "blow it" after you have invested a great deal of yourself in their progress. Sometimes these setbacks can be resolved by your staying steadfastly consistent with the program you have established; other times you may need to modify the program. In either case, consider these setbacks as part of the ADHD student's training and learn to separate yourself from these setbacks.

6. Don't give up! Behavior can change slowly, and the benefits of your efforts may not be seen immediately. Take a long-range view and be optimistic. Your belief in your students will be felt and will make a difference in their lives.

Chapter Nine

Questions and Answers

Is there a "test" for ADHD?

At present, there are no definitive biological tests (e.g., blood tests, brain scans, x-rays) or cognitive tests (e.g., continuous performance tests, computerized tests of learning, IQ tests, achievement tests) that can diagnose ADHD. In addition, it is inappropriate to base a diagnosis of ADHD solely on the child's behavior during a one-time visit to a physician or psychologist. Instead, the diagnosis should be based upon a comprehensive medical and developmental history, interviews and behavior ratings from parents, teachers, and other significant adults in the child's life, review of specific problem areas and symptoms, school records, academic performance measures, and observation of the child's behavior.

Isn't it unfair to reward ADHD students for things that other students do automatically?

Many teachers struggle with this idea. Some believe providing high rates of praise and other rewards is unfair unless all students are rewarded the same way or that providing such rewards is tantamount to reinforcing the problem. Others say that adding reward programs to their classroom takes too much time away from teaching. Still others believe that students should learn through intrinsic or natural rewards such as the excitement in learning new things, getting good grades, or making new friends.

Unfortunately, ADHD students do not usually respond to the typical consequences that work for other students. Many of the rewards in classrooms are too delayed, too weak, or not stimulating enough to motivate an ADHD student. Ordinary reinforcers, such as a teacher's approval or the satisfaction of a job well done, do not stop these children from getting in trouble even

though they know what they are doing is wrong. They are driven by the moment to seek what's stimulating and interesting. This is part of their biological make-up.

To help ADHD students learn to regulate their behavior, block out distractions, and focus on the task at hand, they need frequent, high interest, salient rewards for meeting specific goals. If you are concerned that this practice is unfair, you may be equating fairness with treating all students the same way. Fairness, in an educational sense is probably better defined as treating each student in a manner that affords success for that student (Gordon & Asher, 1994). For the ADHD student, more intense rewards are often what's required.

How do I find the time to praise?

With practice, brief praise takes only a few seconds. Decide on the behaviors you want to praise ahead of time. Then decide on the number of times you want to give praise each period. Use a counter or tally to keep track. Post stickers in your classroom that remind you to praise. If you are spending lots of time attending to negative behavior, you'll find that as you praise more, you probably won't have to spend so much time reprimanding.

What do I do if another student complains because the ADHD student is getting rewards?

If you use individual reward programs, they should be set up privately between you and the child. Using home-based rewards rather than rewards at school helps keep the program private. If other children ask about it, tell them it's something only between you and the child. Most kids understand why the child is being treated differently and also realize the benefits to the class for that child getting along better. Students who are very upset about another student having a reward program are often the ones who would benefit from a program too. Some teachers prefer to use class-wide programs to minimize this problem.

These strategies sound like too much external control. Don't we want to teach self-control?

The first step to teaching self-control is to teach kids to respond to external rules and contingencies. As kids are successful in following these rules, they can gradually be taught methods for inhibiting their own impulses and developing better self-control. However, expect that some external contingencies will always be necessary.

Won't reducing assignments just lead to academic problems or more behavior problems in the future?

Academic problems can result if reducing assignments means the students don't learn the material. To avoid this possibility, make sure you only reduce assignments for those students who already understand the concepts, but who have trouble finishing lengthy assignments. The recommended focus here is on quality, not quantity of work. Assignment reductions are probably most appropriate for students whose inattention and impulsivity are interfering with their ability to complete work. Work reduced for students who are willfully refusing to complete it may reinforce their negative behavior. Remember that these accommodations are meant to provide a mechanism for meeting the special needs of ADHD children and to promote success, enhanced self-esteem, and continued interest in school. If they are not serving that purpose, other interventions should be tried.

What do I do if my token reward system works initially then stops working?

This common problem often occurs because the student has lost interest in the rewards or may be "testing the system." In any case, don't be fooled into thinking that reward systems are ineffective. The target behavior may need to be defined more clearly, the criteria for earning rewards may need to be lowered, consequences may need to be made more consistent or immediate, or alternatively, more powerful rewards may need to be used. These kinds of adjustments are to be expected.

Should we reduce our expectations of ADHD students or excuse their behavior or academic underproductivity because they are unable to do better?

Helping the ADHD child does not mean taking away his or her responsibility to follow rules of behavior, comply with teacher directions, and complete assigned work. However, it does mean helping the child to overcome his or her deficits and obstacles to doing these expected activities. This help includes: increased structure, salience, clarity, and repetition. It also includes increased incentives for following rules and task completion, negative consequences for violations, and decreased expectations of completing assigned work independently without benefit of structure and incentives. Put the structure and incentives in place. Then let the child be responsible for his or her behavior.

References and Readings

Abramowitz, A.J. & O'Leary, S.G. Behavioral interventions for the class room: Implications for students with ADHD. School Psychology Review, 20(2), 220-234, 1991.

Agler, D. Using the goodsport thermometer. Unpublished manuscript, 1995.

American Psychiatric Association. Diagnostic and Statistical Manual of Mental Disorders-Fourth Edition. Washington, DC: American Psychiatric Association, 1994.

Barkley, R.A. Attention Deficit Hyperactivity Disorder: A handbook for diagnosis and treatment, New York: Guilford Press, 1990.

Braswell, L. & Broomquist, M.L. Cognitive-behavioral therapy with ADHD children: Child, family, and school interventions. NY: Guilford Press, 1991.

Cantwell, D.P. Hyperactive children have grown up: What have we learned about what happens to them? Archives of General Psychiatry, 42, 1985.

DuPaul, G.J. & Stoner, G. ADHD in the schools: Assessment and intervention strategies, New York: Guilford Press, 1994.

Gadow, K.D. A school-based medication evaluation program. In J.L. Matson (Ed.), Handbook of hyperactivity in children. Boston: Allyn and Bacon, 1993.

Gordon, S.B. & Asher, M.J. Meeting the ADD challenge: A practical guide for teachers. Illinois: Research Press, 1994.

Hinshaw, S., Henker, B., & Whalen, C. Cognitive-behavioral and pharmacological interventions for hyperactive boys: Comparative and combined

effects. Journal of Consulting and Clinical Psychology, 52, 739-749, 1984.

Kelley, M.L. School-Home Notes: Promoting children's classroom success. New York: Guilford Press, 1990.

Kotkin, R.A. The Irvine Paraprofessional Program: Using paraprofessionals in serving students with ADHD. Intervention in school and clinic, 30, 235-240, 1995.

Kubany E.S., Weiss L.E., & Sloggett B.B. The good behavior clock: A reinforcement/time-out procedure for reducing disruptive classroom behavior. Journal of Behavior Therapy and Experimental Psychiatry, 2, 173-179, 1971.

Lahey, B.B. & Carlson, C.L. Validity of the diagnostic category of Attention Deficit Disorder without Hyperactivity: A review of the literature. Journal of Learning Disabilities, 24, 1991.

McBurnett, K. The new subtype of ADHD: Predominantly Hyperactive-Impulsive. Attention! 1, p. 10-15, 1995.

Pelham, W.E. & Murphy, H.A. Attention deficit and conduct disorders. In M. Ersen (Ed.) Pharmacological and behavioral treatments: An integrative approach. NY: Wiley and Sons, p. 108-148, 1986.

Pfiffner, L.J. & O'Leary, S.G. The efficacy of all-positive management as a function of the prior use of negative consequences. Journal of Applied Behavior Analysis, 20, 1987. (p. 265-271)

Pfiffner, L.J. & O'Leary, S.G. Psychological treatments: School-based. In J.L. Matson (Ed.) Hyperactivity in children: A handbook. Boston: Allyn and Bacon, 234-255, 1993.

Shapiro, & Cole. Self-management interventions for classroom behavior change. New York: Guilford Press, 1994.

Shelton, T. L., & Crosswait, C. Prevention/treatment program for kinder-garten students with ADD. CHADDER, Spring/Summer volume, 1992.

Swanson, J. M. School-based assessments and interventions for ADD students. Irvine, CA: K.C. Publishing, 1992.

Swanson, J.M., McBurnett, L., Christian, D.L., & Wigal, T. Stimulant medications and the treatment of children with ADHD. In T.H. Ollendick & R.J. Prinz (Eds.), Advances in Clinical Child Psychology, 17, 265-322. NY: Plenum Press, 1995

Swanson, J. M.; McBurnett, K.; Wigal, T.; Pfiffner, L.J.; Christian D.; Tamm, L.; Willcutt, E.; Crowley, K.; Clevenger, W.; & Woo, C. The effect of stimulant medication on ADD children: A "review of reviews." Exceptional Children, 60, 154-162, 1993.

Weiss, G. & Hechtman, L.T. Hyperactive children grown-up. NY Guilford Press, 1986.

For Further Reading:

Fowler, M. CH.A.D.D. educators manual: An in-depth look at attention deficit disorders from and educational perspective. Plantation, FL. CH.A.D.D., 1992.

Parker, H.C. The ADD hyperactivity handbook for schools. Plantation FL. Impact Publications Inc. 1992.

Rief, S.F. How to reach and teach ADD/ADHD children: Practical techniques, strategies, and interventions for helping children with atten tion problems and hyperactivity. NY: Simon & Schuster, 1993.

Resources

Parent support groups and national organizations related to ADHD:

Children and Adults with Attention Deficit Disorders (CHADD)
National Headquarters
499 N. W. 70th Avenue, Suite 308
Plantation, Florida 33317
(305) 587-3700

Attention Deficit Disorder Association (ADDA)
P.O. Box 488
West Newbury, MA 01985
(800) 487-2282

Learning Disabilities Association of America (LDAA)
4156 Library Road
Pittsburgh, PA 15234
(412) 341-1515

National Information Center for Children and Youth with Disabilities
(NICHCY)
P.O. Box 1492
Washington, DC 20013-1492
(800) 695-0285

Clearinghouse specializing in the sale of books, tapes, and videos about ADHD for parents, teachers, and children:

ADD Warehouse
300 Northwest 70th Avenue, Suite 102
Plantation, FL 33317
(800) 233-9273

DANEBO ELEMENTARY SCHOOL
1265 CANDLELIGHT DR.
EUGENE, OREGON 97402